The Cherokees

Indians of North America

Heritage Edition

◀ **Indians** ▶
◀ **of North** ▶
◀ **America** ▶

The Cherokees

The Choctaw

The Comanche

The Hopi

The Iroquois

The Mohawk

The Teton Sioux

FIFTY EIGHT

Heritage Edition

◄ Indians ►
◄ of North ►
◄ America ►

The Cherokees

Theda Perdue

Foreword by
Ada E. Deer
University of Wisconsin-Madison

CHELSEA HOUSE
PUBLISHERS
A Haights Cross Communications Company

Philadelphia

The author wishes to thank Julia Coates and others
for their assistance with Chapter 7.

COVER: Basket-weaving has been an integral part of Cherokee society for more
than a thousand years and continues to be a source of pride today.

CHELSEA HOUSE PUBLISHERS

VP, NEW PRODUCT DEVELOPMENT Sally Cheney
DIRECTOR OF PRODUCTION Kim Shinners
CREATIVE MANAGER Takeshi Takahashi
MANUFACTURING MANAGER Diann Grasse

Staff for THE CHEROKEES

EXECUTIVE EDITOR Lee Marcott
EDITOR Christian Green
PRODUCTION EDITOR Noelle Nardone
PHOTO EDITOR Sarah Bloom
SERIES AND COVER DESIGNER Keith Trego
LAYOUT 21st Century Publishing and Communications, Inc.

A Haights Cross Communications ✦ Company

www.chelseahouse.com

First Printing

9 8 7 6 5 4 3 2 1

Library of Congress Cataloging-in-Publication Data

Perdue, Theda, 1949–
  The Cherokees/Theda Perdue.
    p. cm.—(Indians of North America series, revised)
Includes bibliographical references and index.
  ISBN 0-7910-7995-3   0-7910-8347-0 (pbk.)
  1. Cherokee Indians. I. Title. II. Indians of North America, revised.
E99.C5P393 2004
975.004'97557—dc22

                                                    2004004715

Contents

Foreword

Ada E. Deer

American Indians are an integral part of our nation's life and history. Yet most Americans think of their Indian neighbors as stereotypes; they are woefully uninformed about them as fellow humans. They know little about the history, culture, and contributions of Native people. In this new millennium, it is essential for every American to know, understand, and share in our common heritage. The Cherokee teacher, the Mohawk steelworker, and the Ojibwe writer all express their tribal heritage while living in mainstream America.

The revised INDIANS OF NORTH AMERICA series, which focuses on some of the continent's larger tribes, provides the reader with an accurate perspective that will better equip him/her to live and work in today's world. Each tribe has a unique history and culture, and knowledge of individual tribes is essential to understanding the Indian experience.

Prior to the arrival of Columbus in 1492, scholars estimate the Native population north of the Rio Grande ranged from seven to twenty-five million people who spoke more than three hundred different languages. It has been estimated that ninety percent of the Native population was wiped out by disease, war, relocation, and starvation. Today there are more than 567 tribes, which have a total population of more than two million. When Columbus arrived in the Bahamas, the Arawak Indians greeted him with gifts, friendship, and hospitality. He noted their ignorance of guns and swords and wrote they could easily be overtaken with fifty men and made to do whatever he wished. This unresolved clash in perspectives continues to this day.

A holistic view recognizing the connections of all people, the land, and animals pervades the life and thinking of Native people. These core values—respect for each other and all living things; honoring the elders; caring, sharing, and living in balance with nature; and using not abusing the land and its resources— have sustained Native people for thousands of years.

American Indians are recognized in the U.S. Constitution. They are the only group in this country who has a distinctive *political* relationship with the federal government. This relationship is based on the U.S. Constitution, treaties, court decisions, and attorney-general opinions. Through the treaty process, millions of acres of land were ceded *to* the U.S. government *by* the tribes. In return, the United States agreed to provide protection, health care, education, and other services. All 377 treaties were broken by the United States. Yet treaties are the supreme law of the land as stated in the U.S. Constitution and are still valid. Treaties made more than one hundred years ago uphold tribal rights to hunt, fish, and gather.

Since 1778, when the first treaty was signed with the Lenni-Lenape, tribal sovereignty has been recognized and a government-to-government relationship was established. This concept of tribal power and authority has continuously been misunderstood by the general public and undermined by the states. In a series of court decisions in the 1830s, Chief Justice John Marshall described tribes as "domestic dependent nations." This status is not easily understood by most people and is rejected by state governments who often ignore and/or challenge tribal sovereignty. Sadly, many individual Indians and tribal governments do not understand the powers and limitations of tribal sovereignty. An overarching fact is that Congress has plenary, or absolute, power over Indians and can exercise this sweeping power at any time. Thus, sovereignty is tenuous.

Since the July 8, 1970, message President Richard Nixon issued to Congress in which he emphasized "self-determination without termination," tribes have re-emerged and have utilized the opportunities presented by the passage of major legislation such as the American Indian Tribal College Act (1971), Indian Education Act (1972), Indian Education and Self-Determination Act (1975), American Indian Health Care Improvement Act (1976), Indian Child Welfare Act (1978), American Indian Religious Freedom Act (1978), Indian Gaming Regulatory Act (1988), and Native American Graves Preservation and Repatriation Act (1990). Each of these laws has enabled tribes to exercise many facets of their sovereignty and consequently has resulted in many clashes and controversies with the states and the general public. However, tribes now have more access to and can afford attorneys to protect their rights and assets.

Under provisions of these laws, many Indian tribes reclaimed power over their children's education with the establishment of tribal schools and thirty-one tribal colleges. Many Indian children have been rescued from the foster-care system. More tribal people are freely practicing their traditional religions. Tribes with gaming revenue have raised their standard of living with improved housing, schools, health clinics, and other benefits. Ancestors' bones have been reclaimed and properly buried. All of these laws affect and involve the federal, state, and local governments as well as individual citizens.

Tribes are no longer people of the past. They are major players in today's economic and political arenas; contributing millions of dollars to the states under the gaming compacts and supporting political candidates. Each of the tribes in INDIANS OF NORTH AMERICA demonstrates remarkable endurance, strength, and adaptability. They are buying land, teaching their language and culture, and creating and expanding their economic base, while developing their people and making decisions for future generations. Tribes will continue to exist, survive, and thrive.

Ada E. Deer
University of Wisconsin-Madison
June 2004

1

The Principal People

The Cherokees called themselves *Ani'-Yun'wiya*, the "real people" or the "principal people." They lived in a land of high mountains and green valleys, today called the southern Appalachians. The Cherokees believed that their homeland was in the center of the world, and they described the earth as an island suspended by four cords from the sky, which was made of solid rock. Before the island was created, everyone lived above the rock sky, where it was very crowded. The water beetle went down to explore the vast sea beneath the sky. He found no land, but he dived below the water and surfaced with mud that began to grow until it formed the island of the earth. The water beetle returned to the sky and the buzzard went down to see if the island was dry enough for the animals. The buzzard became tired, and his wings began to hit the ground. Everywhere his wings struck the earth, which was still soft, there was a valley, and when he lifted

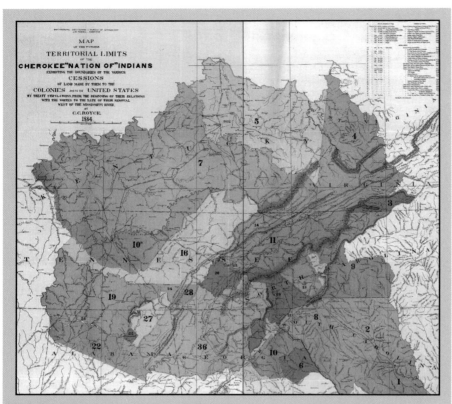

This 1884 map shows the landholdings still held by the Eastern Cherokees—what remained of their original tribal lands at that time.

them, he made a mountain. This is why the Cherokee country is covered with mountains.

At last, the earth was dry enough for plants and animals to come down from the sky. They tried to stay awake but most soon went to sleep. The owl, panther, and a few other animals managed to stay awake for seven days, and as a result, they acquired the power to see in the dark and hunt the animals that sleep. Of the plants, the pine, cedar, spruce, holly, and laurel stayed awake. This is why they stay green year-round instead of losing their leaves in winter like the plants that slept.

The first man and woman were called Kana'ti and Selu. They had only one son until a mysterious child whom they called "Wild Boy" sprang from the river where Selu had washed game. They captured him and tried to tame him, but he remained mischievous.

Kana'ti provided meat for the family. He never failed to bring home deer or turkey when he went hunting in the mountains. One day, the two boys followed their father to see how he had such good luck. He went into the swamp, cut some reeds, and made arrows. Then he climbed a mountainside until he reached a large rock. When he lifted the rock, a fat buck ran out and Kana'ti shot the animal with his arrows.

Several days later, the boys tried to imitate their father. They made arrows and went to the mountain where Kana'ti had killed the game. They lifted the rock, and a deer ran out. They were not quick and skillful like Kana'ti, and before they could shoot that deer, another ran out. In their confusion, they forgot to replace the rock, and all the game escaped. When Kana'ti found out what they had done, he went into the cave, where he found only jars of fleas, lice, bedbugs, gnats, and other vermin. These he released on the boys to punish them. From that day on, Kana'ti had to look for game all over the woods. Sometimes he found food, but sometimes his family had to go hungry.

Selu provided vegetables for the family. She always got corn and beans from the storehouse. One day, the boys spied on her when she went there. They saw her stand in front of a basket rubbing her stomach; suddenly corn appeared in the basket. Then she rubbed her armpits and beans filled the basket. The boys were horrified: Their mother, they decided, was a witch and they must kill her!

Selu knew their intentions. Before she died, she told them to clear the land in front of the cabin, drag her body around the clearing seven times, and stay awake all night. Then there would be plenty of corn in the morning. Because the boys were lazy, they only cleared seven little spots, and they dragged their mother's body over the ground only twice. As a result, corn grew in only a few spots and required cultivation.

The stories about the island and about Kana'ti and Selu were recorded in the late 1800s by anthropologist James Mooney, who visited Cherokees living in North Carolina. The Cherokees told Mooney that these accounts had existed for hundreds of years. They were far more than children's stories, although most Cherokees probably learned them as children. These myths explained why Cherokees lived as they did. All peoples develop explanations for how the world was made, how

Folklore:
How the World Was Made

When the animals and plants were first made—we do not know by whom—they were told to watch and keep awake for seven nights, just as young men now fast and keep awake when they pray to their medicine. They tried to do this, and nearly all were awake through the first night, but the next night several dropped off to sleep, and the third night others were asleep, and then others, until, on the seventh night, of all the animals only the owl, the panther, and one or two more were still awake. To these were given the power to see and to go about in the dark, and to make prey of the birds and animals which must sleep at night. Of the trees only the cedar, the pine, the spruce, the holly, and the laurel were awake to the end, and to them it was given to be always green and to be greatest for medicine, but to the others it was said: "Because you have not endured to the end you shall lose your hair every winter."

Men came after the animals and plants. At first there were only a brother and sister until he struck her with a fish and told her to multiply, and so it was. In seven days a child was born to her, and thereafter every seven days another, and they increased very fast until there was danger that the world could not keep them. Then it was made that a woman should have only one child in a year, and it has been so ever since.

Source: Full text available online at http://creationdays.dk/creationmyth/19.html.

plants and animals acquired their particular characteristics, how the first people lived, and how their own society came into being. The stories Mooney wrote down explained how the principal people's world had developed.

For the Cherokees, the mountains that the buzzard made had been their home for at least a thousand years when Europeans first arrived in their villages in 1540. Western North Carolina was the heart of the Cherokee homeland, but in the early years of European contact, they also lived in what are today up-country South Carolina, northern Georgia, northeastern Alabama, and eastern Tennessee.

The Cherokees lived in villages that sometimes stretched for several miles along riverbanks. Each village had a council house (or town house) and a plaza where the villagers met to socialize, make political decisions, and conduct religious cere-monies. The council house was a very large circular building that sometimes sat atop an earthen mound. The walls of the council house were constructed of wattle (interwoven saplings) and then covered with daub (a plaster of mud). Benches lined the walls, and a fire smoldered in a central hearth. There were no windows and only a small opening for a door. The council house opened onto a plaza that was surrounded by covered sheds, where villagers sat during warm summer weather to watch events such as games, dances, and ceremonies.

Beyond the council house and plaza lay private houses. A Cherokee household was large: it often included several genera-tions. Therefore, Cherokee homesteads consisted of a variety of buildings. In the summer, Cherokees lived in large, rectangular, clapboard houses. In the winter, they moved into their *asi*, or winter houses, which were small, round, wattle-and-daub structures. The fire constantly smoldering in the hearth made the windowless asi dark and smoky. Households also had storage buildings and cribs, similar to Selu's storehouse.

Unlike Selu, Cherokees could not rely on magic to fill their baskets with corn and beans. Instead, they planted, tended, and harvested the crops by hand. Each household had its own small garden, but most food came from large fields that the villagers farmed communally. These fields lay in the fertile river valleys where corn grew well. The Cherokees planted their corn and beans together in hills: The bean vines ran up the cornstalks and the nitrogen naturally produced by beans fertilized the corn. Between these hills, the people grew squash, sunflowers, pumpkins, and other crops.

Like Selu, women were responsible for providing vegetables. Men helped with clearing fields, planting, and harvesting, but the chief responsibility for agriculture fell to the women. They hoed the crops with stone implements or pointed digging sticks. Old women, who could not perform such heavy physical labor, helped by sitting on scaffolds in the middle of fields and chasing away crows and raccoons that tried to raid the crops. When the corn was edible, the women presented it to the village in the Cherokees' most important ritual, the *Green Corn Ceremony*. (For additional information on this ceremony and other Cherokee ceremonies, enter "Cherokee ceremonies" into any search engine and browse the many sites listed.)

While they were busy in the fields, women also had to tend to their children. Because they lived in extended families, which included several mothers with children of different ages as well as older women, Cherokee women could share the task of child rearing. They often took children to the fields with them. Those old enough to help did so. Infants were bound to a cradleboard, a kind of portable crib, and mothers left them in the shade of a tree or perhaps even hanging from a low bough.

The Cherokees were very lenient with their children. Parents never spanked their offspring; the only physical punishment used was lightly scratching disobedient youngsters with thorns. The indulgence demonstrated by Selu, who provided for her children although she knew they were about to kill her, represented the tolerant spirit among Cherokees. Naughty children were often shamed into good behavior with teasing, which was supposed to embarrass them into mending their ways.

Women not only cared for children and farmed but also gathered firewood, carried water, and cooked food. Cherokees did not have regular meals and instead ate whenever they were hungry. Their favorite food was corn, which they prepared in many different ways. The Cherokees allowed most corn to ripen and dry in the fields. Then they soaked the hard kernels in water mixed with wood ashes (lye), a solution that removed the husk. Women pounded the corn kernels in a mortar made from a tree trunk with a wooden pestle, which had a large end to give it weight. When they had finished pounding, they sifted the corn to separate the chunks from the fine meal. The chunks were used in soups and stews. The cornmeal was used for bread. Breads also included other ingredients, such as dried beans and chestnuts. Cherokees had no butter, but they used bear grease or the oil from pounded nuts on their bread.

The task of furnishing Cherokee houses fell to the women, who employed a variety of materials and techniques. They crafted benches for sleeping and sitting from saplings and made baskets, which had many uses, from river cane, a kind of native bamboo. The Cherokees constructed some baskets with two layers of woven river cane; the double weaving gave them extra strength. Women created dyes from bloodroot, butternut, walnut, and other plants to decorate their baskets with unusual designs. After contact with Europeans, women began to make baskets out of maple, oak, and honeysuckle as well.

Pottery was made from native clay. The Cherokees had no potter's wheel so women coiled their pots from long ropes of clay. Then they smoothed the sides with a stone and stamped or cut a design into the outside. The unglazed pots were put in open fires to harden and thus acquired a dark black finish that reminded Europeans of cast iron.

Cherokee women also helped men dress deerskins and then fashioned the skins into clothes using needles made of bone. Sewing for the family was not a difficult task because Cherokees normally had few clothes. In fact, children usually wore nothing at all. Women donned a short skirt, as did men. In the winter, they might add a skin cloak and moccasins that laced up to their knees. Women and children spent the cold months inside the winter house, where they were warm despite their scanty clothing. Both men and women were fond of jewelry and wore necklaces of shell, bone, and copper.

Men and women may have worn similar clothing, but they lived very separate lives. While women farmed, cared for children, cooked, made household goods, and did other domestic chores, men contributed to their family's livelihood by hunting. Like Kana'ti, men were responsible for providing their family with meat. The Cherokees kept no livestock before the arrival of Europeans, and so all meat was wild game—deer, bear, and turkey in particular. Winter was the season for hunting, and a hunting party would often be gone for several months in search of game. Cherokees hunted as far west as the Mississippi River and perhaps even beyond.

Deer was the most important game animal. The Cherokees ate the deer's flesh, tanned the animal's hide using a solution distilled from deer brains, wore the skins, made tools and ornaments from bones and antlers, and used sinews for thread and hooves for glue. They tried not to waste anything. The same was true with the bear and turkey. Cherokees prized bears for their thick fur and for their fat, which they rendered into grease. Bear claws doubled as jewelry. Turkeys provided not only meat but also feathers for personal adornment. The Cherokees used feather wands in ceremonial dances and fashioned capes from feathers by affixing them to a netting made of bark strips.

Cherokee men used bows and arrows to kill large game such as deer. They made points for their arrows by chipping flint or other stones or by carving bone. Sometimes they used traps to capture bears. Birds and rabbits fell victim to smaller traps. Cherokees also used blowguns and darts to kill these animals. In fact, a boy had to demonstrate his mastery of the blowgun before he could advance to using a bow and arrow.

The Cherokees had several techniques for catching fish. They had hooks and nets as well as traps. Perhaps the most effective way of obtaining a fish dinner, however, was to poison a stream. The Cherokees built a dam across the stream and then stirred an organic poison such as ground horse chestnuts into the water. The poison attacked the nervous system of the fish but caused no harm to the humans who ate them. The paralyzed fish floated to the surface, and the fishermen simply selected the ones they wanted. When the dam was opened and fresh water diluted the poison, the other fish recovered and swam away.

When men were not hunting, they spent much of their time playing games that improved their coordination and kept them physically fit for war and long winter hunts. Men held arrow-shooting contests, tossed shafts at a rolling stone disk, and played stickball. Stickball, similar to modern lacrosse, was more than a mere game. Played by two teams with equal numbers of participants, stickball was called "the little brother to war." Players wielded one or two wooden rackets and hurled a hard deerskin ball up and down the field, trying to cross the opponent's goal line. Preparation for the game involved some of the same rituals as going to war, such as fasting and scratching the skin, and like warriors, stickball players some-times sustained serious injuries. Villagers had great enthusiasm for these games and often wagered on them.

Men always seemed to be hunting, fishing, or playing games, which Europeans considered enjoyable leisure activities, while women farmed, conforming to European ideas of menial labor. Interpreting Cherokee practices according to European cultural assumptions, which regarded women as subservient and inferior to men, Europeans decided that lazy Cherokee men dominated and exploited women. Nothing could have been further from the truth. Although Cherokee women worked very hard, they also had enormous power and authority that made them subservient to no one.

The prominent role women played in society stemmed in part from the Cherokees' *matrilineal* kinship system. In such a kinship system, people trace their descent through women instead of men or, as we do in our culture, through both men and women. Cherokees belonged to their mother's *clan*, a group tracing its descent from a common ancestor. In Cherokee society, a person's only clan relatives were those on the mother's side. Relatives included a person's mother and the mother's mother, sisters, sisters' children, and brothers (but not her brothers' children). In other words, the Cherokees did not consider a child related by blood to the father or to the father's mother, sisters, and brothers.

In the Cherokee kinship system, there were seven clans, each of which bore a special name: Wolf, Deer, Bird, Paint, Long Hair, Blind Savannah, or Holly. (The translations of the last three are uncertain.) These clans were scattered throughout Cherokee country. Every village probably had households representing each of the clans, and so a Cherokee could always find relatives in a village even if he had never been there before. Therefore, the matrilineal clan system served to unite the Cherokees.

The Cherokees were matrilocal as well as matrilineal; that is, a family lived in the household of the mother. A man resided with his wife and children in a household that usually included her mother, her sisters, her sisters' children and husbands, and her unmarried brothers. If husband and wife divorced, as they did frequently in Cherokee society, the husband simply moved out of his wife's household and into the house of his mother and sisters. Children always stayed with their mother because, after all, they were not considered the clan kin of their father.

Children, of course, knew who their father was. They loved and respected him. The man who trained boys to hunt and decided when they were old enough to go to war, however, was not their father but their mother's brother, their uncle. He was the man to whom boys and girls owed their greatest respect. The mother's family, in other words, controlled the lives of children—another factor that probably contributed to women's prestige in Cherokee society.

Women not only held power within the family, but they also wielded influence within the village. In the village council, the traditional form of Cherokee government, prominent female members of the community freely voiced their opinions, as did well-respected men. Council meetings were run democratically; villagers debated an issue until they reached consensus. This model was repeated throughout the Cherokee homeland, in which individual settlements governed them-selves—neither a chief nor a national council ruled the tribe as a whole until the late eighteenth century. Government did not unify the Cherokees. Instead, a common language (although there were three or four dialects), the kinship system, and shared beliefs made the Cherokees one people.

One of the most serious questions a town council had to deliberate was whether or not to go to war. The Cherokees did not fight for territory or out of patriotism. The only reason they went to war was to avenge the deaths of Cherokees who had been killed by an enemy. The spirits of the dead could not go to the "darkening land," where they were supposed to dwell after death, until their relatives had taken revenge on their killers. The enemy could be the English, Spanish, French, or other Native Americans, such as the Creeks, Shawnees, Senecas, or Chickasaws. The council determined who was responsible for Cherokee fatalities and rallied support for a war party.

The size of war parties ranged from two or three to more than a hundred, but expeditions normally involved between twenty and forty warriors. Clan members of those killed had a special obligation to avenge their relatives' death, and so they were the Cherokees most likely to join a war party. The decision to go to war was strictly up to an individual. If a warrior experienced uneasiness or suffered from nightmares about a particular expedition, he was thought to be receiving bad omens and was encouraged to remain at home. The Cherokees applauded anyone who had the good sense to pay attention to these signs.

The men who decided to participate in a raid assembled in the council house to prepare for battle. The Cherokees believed that victory would come only if warriors were spiritually pure, and so the men seeking vengeance fasted, drank *black drink* (a special tea containing lots of caffeine), took emetics in order to vomit and thus cleanse themselves, and participated in rituals designed to ensure victory. They followed this regimen for several days.

When the warriors left the village, they took great care to avoid detection and ambush. They traveled single file, and each warrior stepped into the footprint of the warrior in front of him. Sometimes they attached bear paws to their feet and followed the course bears might take in order to trick the enemy. The warriors concealed their presence by camouflaging themselves and imitating the sounds of the forest. They often communicated by whistling birdcalls or vocalizing other animal noises. The warriors wanted to take the enemy by surprise, quietly and quickly, and then withdraw. Sometimes pitched battles took place, but the Cherokees preferred the safety of ambush.

Because their objective was vengeance, the warriors hoped enemy casualties would equal the number of Cherokees who had been killed. Once they had taken the required lives, they went home. Eventually, the enemy would come for vengeance against the Cherokees but for the time being, the war was over. For the Cherokees and their Indian neighbors, war was not a series of campaigns with a single goal and ultimate victory or defeat but rather a series of continuing raids. The Cherokees retaliated for an attack by the enemy, who then sought vengeance on the Cherokees, who once again retaliated. War was never ending.

Sometimes Cherokees captured some of the enemy. The fate of these captives rested with War Women. War Women accompanied many war parties to cook food and carry firewood and water, and some had distinguished themselves in battle. Nancy Ward was a War Woman of the Wolf clan who lived in the late eighteenth century. Later in life, she married trader Brian Ward and anglicized her name, but as a young woman, she was married to the warrior Kingfisher. She accompanied his war party, probably as cook and water carrier, on a raid against the Creeks. When Kingfisher was killed in battle, she seized his gun, rallied the Cherokees, and led her people to victory. The Cherokees honored her, as they had other women who demonstrated such bravery, with the title "War Woman," which gave her power over captives.

Although Cherokee clans usually adopted children and female captives, the War Women usually condemned warriors to the stake. In vengeance for their dead relatives, village women took charge of the torture, and they beat and burned victims, sometimes for several days, before they died. This practice seems horrifying today, but it made sense in terms of the Cherokee belief that spirits of the dead rested only when their deaths had been avenged. Unlike war, in which mostly men participated, torture gave all Cherokees an opportunity to help send the spirits of their deceased relatives to the darkening land.

Vengeance was also important to Cherokees because they believed that they must keep the world in balance, in a state of equilibrium. When a Cherokee died, the world was out of balance until the person responsible for that death also died. The Cherokees thought that if they did not maintain equilibrium, then droughts, storms, disease, or other disasters might occur. Cherokees believed that the principal people's major purpose was to keep the world in harmony and balance.

This view of their role in the world helps explain the Cherokee judicial system. The Cherokees had no police or law courts. If a person wronged another, it was up to the injured person's clan to obtain retribution or vengeance. Murder, of course, was the most serious crime. If one Cherokee killed another, the world was out of kilter just as it would have been if the Cherokee had been killed by an enemy. In order to reestablish the balance, the murderer or a member of the murderer's clan had to die. Normally, the murderer surrendered, because otherwise an innocent relative was likely to suffer the penalty for the crime. The murderer's kin did not offer protection, although sometimes an uncle or other close kin might volunteer instead to suffer the murderer's fate. Nor did the clan retaliate for the death of a murderer or his/her substitute. The death of a member of the killer's clan restored harmony and balance.

The Cherokees' concern for harmony was evident in many areas of their life. Selu and Kana'ti, the providers of vegetables and meat, complemented each other. By hunting, men balanced women, who farmed. Summer, the season for farming, complemented winter, the season for hunting. Thus, Cherokees took care to do things in the appropriate season to preserve order.

Because the principal people sought to maintain harmony and balance in the world, they tried not to exploit nature. When a hunter killed a deer, for example, he performed a special ritual in which he apologized to the spirit of the deer and explained that his family needed food. Hunters never killed for sport. They believed that if they violated their sacred trust, terrible things would happen to them. The exploitation of animals could bring disease. If this happened, plants, which were a natural counterbalance to animals, could provide a cure.

Cherokee religion centered on sustaining harmony. At the Green Corn Ceremony, the Cherokees tried to wipe out any disorder that had crept in during the year and begin anew.

At this time, villagers cleaned private houses and the council house, threw away broken baskets and pottery, discarded any food left over from the preceding year, and extinguished old fires in a ceremonial gesture of renewal. The women presented the village with new corn, which had just become edible, and prepared a great feast. The Cherokees also dissolved unhappy marriages at this time and forgave all old wrongs except murder. People began the year with a clean slate and the knowledge that order had been restored.

Because the Cherokees killed game only when they needed it and destroyed any surplus at the Green Corn Ceremony, they never accumulated wealth. In fact, they strongly disapproved of anyone who tried to produce more than was needed to survive. This trait amazed early European visitors but it probably contributed to the Cherokees' generous hospitality, which Europeans also noted. The Cherokees had no real reason to impress each other or anyone else with worldly goods. They were, after all, the principal people, the descendants of Kana'ti and Selu. They lived in the center of the island that was the world, and they protected that world by maintaining harmony and order.

2

Cherokees and Europeans

The principal people, living in the center of their island, were certainly no strangers to change. Their way of life had evolved over thousands of years. Distant ancestors had survived by hunting big-game animals that are long extinct; more recent ancestors had given up a nomadic existence for village life and farming. The development of agriculture had altered Cherokee society, and the rate of change accelerated with the introduction of corn, about one thousand years before Europeans first encountered the Cherokees. As significant as these innovations were, they probably were imperceptible to the Cherokees because they took place over such a long period of time. In contrast, the cultural changes that accompanied the arrival of Europeans were rapid, dramatic, and painfully obvious. Europeans threatened the Cherokees not only physically but also culturally and socially.

The Cherokees first came into contact with Europeans in 1540. Hernando de Soto, a Spanish conquistador, passed through Cherokee territory on his exploration of what is now the southeastern United States. De Soto traveled with a large entourage of soldiers, horses, pigs, and Native people whom he had enslaved to carry the expedition's supplies. He was looking for gold and silver or other forms of wealth that he could send home to Spain. He was disappointed with what he found in the Southeast. He found no grand cities or rich mines such as those Spanish explorers had discovered in Mexico and Peru.

Instead, de Soto encountered farmers living in towns with populations ranging from hundreds to thousands. Even large communities, such as the fortified town he found in present-day Alabama, had no sumptuous palaces filled with riches. Reluctant to accept the truth that the Indians had no gold, de Soto's soldiers tried to force Natives to reveal the whereabouts of their nonexistent mines. Many people, unable to do so, died. Others became slaves of the Spaniards, and they acted as guides or translators, or carried supplies for the expedition. Subsequent Spanish expeditions, such as that of Juan Pardo in the 1560s, may have discovered small natural deposits of precious metals, but these early attempts to exploit the Indians and their resources were not very successful.

Spanish and later expeditions had a particularly devastating effect on the Cherokees and other Native peoples through an unseen and, at the time, unknown force—disease. Many diseases that afflicted Europeans did not exist in America. Because a vast ocean separated Europe and America, Indians had built up no natural immunities to European diseases, which thrived in urban centers fouled by domestic animals. These diseases included the great killers such as smallpox and bubonic plague and diseases such as measles, a virus from which most European sufferers quickly recovered. When an Indian contracted a European disease, however, his or her chance of survival was far slimmer than those of an afflicted European. Measles, to say nothing of smallpox and the plague, became a deadly disease for Native Americans.

The organisms that carried these diseases often spread ahead of European explorers. De Soto encountered villages that had been hit by epidemics shortly before his arrival. Some appeared to have been totally wiped out. In a single epidemic in 1738, one-third of the Cherokees died of smallpox. Modern demographers, those who study population shifts, debate mortality rates. Some theorize that the first hundred years of European presence in America brought about the demise of ninety-five percent of the Native population, while others suggest that a death rate of seventy-five percent may be more accurate. They agree, however, that disease was a major factor in this depopulation. They also agree that the long-term effects of epidemics were both cultural and demographic. Disease disproportionately claimed the very old and the very young. Disease robbed Indians of their past. When the elderly died, they carried to the grave many oral traditions, sacred formulas, and lifetimes of knowledge that they had not completely transferred to younger generations. The death of children threatened the future of Indian communities because populations lost not only the individuals who died but also the children they could have expected to have if they had grown up.

Cherokees probably did not associate the new deadly diseases with Europeans. They believed that misfortune came about when the world was out of balance, and they turned to their priests to restore balance. The priests, medicine men and women, presumably knew what plants to use and words to say to cure disease. Many of these new ailments, however, seemed to be beyond their power, and they could not cure the European diseases or stop their progress. This must have produced doubts about the priests and their medicine. There is a Cherokee story about the people rising up and killing priests who had violated custom. We do not know whether the story is true or not, but it suggests that, at some point, Cherokees began to question some of their traditional beliefs. The old remedies did not work for the new conditions that the principal people confronted.

Unlike Native peoples living along the coast, the Cherokees had some time to cope with the initial effects of European contact before large numbers of Europeans came to their country. Spain's rivals, France and England, began to challenge Spanish claims to North America in the late sixteenth century but few Europeans ventured into Cherokee country again for more than a century. In these largely unknown decades, the Cherokees probably reorganized themselves politically and, because their population grew in relation to their neighbors who had been hit even harder by disease, they may have expanded into new territory across the mountains in what is today East Tennessee. By the early eighteenth century, they had attracted the attention of English traders from Virginia and Carolina, who traveled to their territory occasionally. Spanish Florida and French Louisiana also had imperial ambitions that included the Cherokees. We know relatively little about the response of the Cherokees and other Native peoples to these early Europeans. We can speculate, however, how they might have regarded these invaders.

The Cherokees, of course, knew that there were people other than the principal people living in the world. They had both traded with and sent war parties against Creeks, Choctaws, and Chickasaws to the south and the Iroquois to the north. These people were different from the principal people, and in one of their dances, the *Booger Dance*, the Cherokees made fun of what they saw as the peculiarities of these other Indians. When Europeans arrived, the Cherokees incorporated them into the Booger Dance and depicted them as physically and sexually aggressive: The Indian playing the part of the European chased screaming girls around the dance ground. The Cherokees had no concept of race or of racial solidarity. They did not see other Native Americans as more closely related to them than Europeans. Europeans were simply a different and particularly aggressive people.

Traders were the first Europeans whom the Cherokees came to know well. Traders not only wanted to sell the Indians a variety of European manufactured goods, such as metal farming implements, but they also wanted to buy deerskins, which were an important source of leather in Europe at this time. At first, traders came to the Cherokee country in late winter or early spring, when the men were returning with skins from the winter hunt. They exchanged the goods they had brought by packhorse from the English colonies for the skins, which they loaded on horses for the return journey.

By the early eighteenth century, traders were beginning to build stores in the Cherokee country and to live there year-round. Many of them married Cherokee women. A Cherokee wife helped make the trader a part of the Cherokee community. He could learn her native language from her or she could be his interpreter. Furthermore, his children by her were Cherokees: That is, in the Cherokees' matrilineal kinship system, the children of Cherokee mothers were Cherokees regardless of the race of the father.

Intermarriage with Cherokee women challenged but did not entirely subvert traditional Cherokee social organization. The women came to live with their husbands, contrary to the Cherokee custom of husbands residing with their wives. These women, however, often considered their husbands' houses and business to be theirs, in accord with custom. Children took their father's name, and they inherited their father's houses, stores, and goods. They often spoke English as well as Cherokee, received some education, and adopted some of the beliefs and customs of Europeans. But they also inherited their mother's clan affiliation, which made them full-fledged tribal members, and her family had a major role in their upbringing. Since traders normally married the sisters or nieces of chiefs, their children had traditional Cherokee claims on powerful positions once they reached adulthood.

The traders who lived in the Cherokee country obtained goods to barter with in Charleston, South Carolina, or some other port city. At the end of hunting season, they shipped back the skins that Cherokee hunters sold them. By living in the Indian community, however, they could sell to their customers throughout the year, not just in the spring as the itinerant traders had. These traders extended credit to hunters against the skins they would bring in the spring. In this way, many Indians became indebted to the traders.

Cherokees also gradually became dependent on the goods the traders provided them, especially metal tools such as hoes or knife blades, which the Cherokees found far superior to traditional stone tools. Two other commodities, guns and ammunition, quickly became necessities for protecting the principal people from their enemies who were also armed. As the Cherokees used more and more of these European products, they abandoned their own crafts: People forgot how to chip a stone knife and lost much of their skill with the bow and arrow. Trade with Europeans became a necessity rather than a luxury.

At the same time, European demand for skins increased. Traders raised prices for manufactured goods, and Indians had little choice but to provide more skins. In their renewed efforts to obtain more skins, hunters began to abandon their traditional attitude toward killing deer and their concern for keeping the world in balance. The number of deer they took increased dramatically. In 1708, for example, the Cherokees sold fifty thousand skins to traders; by 1735, deerskin sales totaled one million.

In addition to deerskins, traders bought war captives from Cherokees. These captives were Indians of other tribes whom the Cherokees had captured. Traditionally, most of them would have been tortured or killed, but traders offered to buy them. Warriors relinquished their captives to traders, who sent them to Charleston, where they were sold as slaves. These Indian slaves worked alongside African slaves on rice and tobacco plantations in the American colonies or on sugar plantations in the West Indies. As Cherokees and other Indians discovered the European market for captives, warfare increased and was motivated by the desire to take prisoners rather than the wish to gain vengeance.

Successful hunters and warriors achieved a new prominence in Cherokee society as the primary providers of European trade goods. Women who had previously enjoyed considerable freedom became dependent on men for such things as hoes, kettles, and even clothing, because men sold the skins that previously had served as clothing. The new economic power obtained by hunters and warriors brought an increased political power. Because others relied on them, their opinions in council began to carry more weight than those who did not have deerskins and captives to sell to the traders. This political power grew stronger when Europeans began to enlist Indian warriors to help fight their wars in North America.

The Cherokees became embroiled in the European struggle for North America in the eighteenth century. The Spanish held Florida; the French controlled Canada, the Mississippi River valley, and Louisiana; the British occupied the Atlantic seaboard. Each foreign nation wanted to dominate North America and sought Indian allies to help them. The Cherokees were never seriously tempted to aid the Spanish, who were too far away, but the British and French competed for Cherokee allegiance. Although the Cherokees usually sided with the British, many did transfer their allegiance to the French during the course of the Seven Years' War (1754–1763).

At the beginning of this conflict—also called the French and Indian War—the Cherokees supported the English. Choctaw and Iroquois allies of the French repeatedly attacked Cherokee towns, and so the Cherokees asked the British to build forts and station soldiers in their territory to protect their homes and families. In 1756, the English built Fort Prince George in what is now South Carolina and Fort Loudoun in eastern Tennessee.

After the completion of the forts, the Cherokees agreed to accompany the English on a campaign against the French and their Shawnee allies in the Ohio River valley. Heavy snows and swollen rivers cost the warriors their horses and provisions and forced them to turn back after six weeks. By the time they reached the Virginia frontier, the warriors desperately needed food. They happened upon some cows that were grazing in the woods. The warriors regarded the unpenned livestock as game and appropriated the cattle for food. When the English farmers who owned the livestock discovered their loss, they attacked the Cherokees, killed several, and took their scalps. Adding insult to injury, the Englishmen then claimed that the scalps belonged to enemy Indians and sold them to the Virginia legislature, which had offered a reward for such prizes.

When word of the attack reached Cherokee country, young warriors began to avenge the deaths of their relatives by raiding English settlements. Older headmen tried to restrain them and even sent a delegation to Charleston in 1758 to arrange a truce between the Cherokees and the British colonists. However, the raids continued. In November 1759, thirty-two of the most prominent Cherokee leaders assembled at Fort Prince George to work out an acceptable agreement with the South Carolina colonial governor.

The governor ignored the peaceful nature of their visit to the fort and imprisoned the entire party in a room intended for six soldiers. In exchange for the chiefs, the governor demanded the surrender of all Cherokees who had killed Englishmen and all Frenchmen who lived in Cherokee towns. A few concessions by the Cherokees prompted the governor to release the war chief Oconostota and two others. In February 1760, Oconostota laid siege to Fort Prince George. After several weeks, he sent word that he wanted a conference with the fort's commander. When the lieutenant in charge stepped from the stockade, Oconostota signaled his warriors to attack. Immediately, the soldiers inside the fort burst into the room where they held the Cherokee hostages and massacred the twenty-nine unarmed chiefs. (For additional information on Oconostota, enter

Cunne Shote, also known as Oconostota, was a Cherokee war leader, probably the most powerful individual member of the Cherokee tribe between 1760 and 1782. Besides leading his people in war, he was a diplomat who established alliances with both the English and the French.

"Cherokee Chief Oconostota" into any search engine and browse the many sites listed.)

In retaliation, the Cherokees accelerated their attacks along the Carolina frontier and placed Fort Loudoun under siege. In June 1760, Colonel Archibald Montgomery and sixteen hundred soldiers invaded Cherokee territory. They destroyed all the lower towns, located on the banks of the Savannah River, in what is now Georgia, slaughtered more than a hundred Cherokees, and drove the homeless survivors into the mountains. Montgomery then advanced toward the middle towns on the banks of the Little Tennessee and Tuckaseigee Rivers. On June 27, the Cherokees halted his progress near the present-day state line separating North and South Carolina. A large force of warriors ambushed the company, cut down nearly a hundred Englishmen, and forced Montgomery to retreat to Fort Prince George.

The defeat of Montgomery's force doomed Fort Loudoun. Cut off from help, the soldiers had to eat their dogs and horses. On August 8, the garrison surrendered. The Cherokees agreed to conduct their prisoners to the English settlements if they turned over all their guns and ammunition. The soldiers, however, buried most of their weapons or threw them in the river. This dishonesty sealed their fate: The next day at dawn, the Cherokees struck, killing thirty of the soldiers and taking the survivors captive.

The next summer, the English launched another expedition against the Cherokees. This time a force of twenty-six hundred men including a number of Chickasaw and Choctaw warriors defeated the Cherokees. Following the example of Montgomery, the soldiers destroyed fifteen middle towns. British lieutenant Francis Marion described a typical day of the campaign in his journal:

We proceeded, by Colonel [James] Grant's orders, to burn the Indian cabins. Some of the men seemed to enjoy this cruel work, laughing heartily at the flames, but to me it appeared a shocking sight. Poor creatures, thought I, we surely need not grudge you such miserable habitations. But when we came, according to orders, to cut down the fields of corn, I could scarcely refrain from tears. Who, without grief, could see the stately stalks with broad green leaves and tasseled shocks, the staff of life, sink under our swords with all their precious load. . . . I saw everywhere around the footsteps of the little Indian children, where they had lately played under the shade of their rustling corn. When we are gone, thought I, they will return, and peeping through the weeds with tearful eyes, will mark the ghastly ruin where they had so often played.

Famine resulted from the destruction of the corn crop and lowered the Cherokees' resistance to disease; a smallpox epidemic followed. According to some estimates, war, hunger, and disease reduced the Cherokee population to half its prewar total.

The Cherokees lost a considerable amount of territory after the war because Europeans required the defeated Indian tribes to relinquish land. In 1770, a *treaty* deprived the Cherokees of their hunting grounds in Virginia and present-day West Virginia. In 1772, the Cherokees surrendered the territory east of the Kentucky River, and in 1775, in a fraudulent land transaction, they "sold" their land to the west of that river. The loss of their primary hunting grounds following the Seven Years' War added to the economic distress the Cherokees were suffering as a result of the ruin of their towns and fields.

The Cherokees lost the Seven Years' War, but they and other Indian peoples had inflicted serious casualties on the English colonists. Therefore, the British Crown attempted to appease Native peoples and listened to their complaints, which centered around their resentment of colonists who illegally occupied Indian land. In order to remove this source of friction, the British tried to halt the westward movement of their colonists by prohibiting settlement beyond the Appalachian Mountains. Although some English settlers violated this proclamation, the Indians recognized it as an attempt by the Crown to prevent mistreatment of Native peoples. This was one reason why most Cherokees sided with the British during the American Revolution (1775–1783). Encouraged by British agents and aided by

Tories—colonists who took the side of the British Crown during the American War of Independence—the Cherokees raided the frontiers of Georgia, Virginia, and the Carolinas in the summer of 1776. The rebellious colonists retaliated with a four-pronged invasion. The Cherokees, who still had not recovered from the Seven Years' War, were able to offer only minor resistance. The American soldiers remembered well how close the Cherokees had come to victory in 1760 and how frontier communities had suffered from raids. They intended to punish the Cherokees.

General Griffith Rutherford, who commanded the North Carolina troops, was determined to demolish every one of the middle towns. The soldiers killed and scalped women as well as men, and they sold children into slavery. The Cherokees who escaped fled to the mountains where they were exposed to the elements and subsisted on whatever wild foods they could find. Altogether, more than fifty towns were destroyed, most of them by Rutherford, and their residents were left without food or shelter.

The Cherokees recovered economically from the destruction of their towns but suffered long-lasting psychological trauma from the violence they had experienced. Twenty years after Rutherford's campaign, U.S. Indian agent Benjamin Hawkins discovered that when he rode into some Cherokee villages, the women were mute with fear. The children, who had heard of Rutherford's expedition from their parents and grandparents, screamed in terror at the mere sight of a white man and hid until he left their village.

After the American Revolution, the majority of Cherokees favored peace and agreed to give up all lands east of the Appalachians. But a small band of warriors, called "Chickamaugas," was unwilling to accept a truce and moved their families to northeastern Alabama. With the assistance of the Spanish in Louisiana, they continued to fight until 1794. The Chickamaugas feared that the expansion of the United States spelled doom for the Cherokees and believed that by engaging in war, they were protecting their territory the only way they could. The might of the United States, and particularly the Tennesseans, proved too great, however, and the Chickamaugas were forced to surrender after their towns were destroyed. Some chose to move west but most decided to try to live in peace with white Americans.

The warfare of the eighteenth century brought change to the Cherokee political structure. Europeans did not want to deal with councils that deliberated at length over issues of war and peace. When Europeans needed warriors to accompany their military campaigns, they did not like to participate in debates; they wanted the warriors *immediately*. Therefore, they gave gifts of guns, ammunition, textiles, tools, and other goods to prominent warriors who could provide them with manpower. Europeans recognized these men as chiefs, and they came to exercise unprecedented power in Cherokee society because they distributed European goods to other warriors who were willing to go into battle, thus serving as a primary link between the Cherokees and the whites. The responsibility for enforcing treaties and alliances fell to the war chiefs.

The warriors came to share political dominance with the descendants of traders, many of whom also were warriors. Traders and warriors were the people with whom non-Indians interacted, and the most important political questions facing the Cherokees in the late eighteenth century concerned non-Indians. For the Cherokees, this meant important changes. Instead of a council of all people making decisions for each town independently, a few individuals made and enforced decisions.

Most Cherokees did not object. They recognized that in their situation, they needed to delegate political power; someone had to be spokesperson for the Cherokees, but they expected that person, or persons, to be accountable to them. Only if they had clearly designated officials could they prevent unauthorized sales of land. These officials also needed to enforce treaties and other laws to protect the people from retaliation for actions of a few. Individual Cherokees gave up some of their freedom and independence; and they believed that, in return, they had gained a degree of security for the principal people and their homeland.

3

Cherokee "Civilization"

In the late eighteenth and early nineteenth centuries, the Cherokees faced a period of rebirth and regeneration—a renaissance. At the end of the American Revolution, the Cherokees faced a severe economic depression. They had to relinquish large tracts of territory to the United States that included village sites as well as hunting grounds. The displaced people relocated but many chose to live in isolated homesteads, less attractive to invaders, rather than in towns. The whole fabric of Cherokee society seemed to be disintegrating. The Cherokees, however, proved to be incredibly adaptive. While retaining many traditional customs, values, and beliefs, they selectively adopted some of the ways of life of white Americans. The Cherokees hoped that if they embraced some cultural changes, they could survive as a people in their homeland.

The new U.S. government aided the Cherokees in this transformation because the leaders saw that it was to their advantage for the

Cherokees to give up the hunting and warfare that traditionally had been crucial to Indian culture. Convincing Indians to abandon warfare was essential to the new nation's survival because the United States was very weak in its early years. Already involved in an Indian war north of the Ohio River, the nation could not afford an Indian war in the South, too. Furthermore, some wanted the United States to expand, and they viewed the Indian hunting grounds as potential farms for white pioneers. If Indians gave up hunting, they would have no use for hunting grounds and could be induced to sell this "surplus" land to the United States. In that way, the United States would obtain Indian land without a costly war.

Although U.S. officials had ulterior motives, some of the individuals involved truly wanted to help the Indians. They believed that only acceptance of the white people's way of life would save Indians from destruction. In order to save the Indians, the U.S. government developed a policy to "civilize" them. A "civilized" society, policymakers believed, was one composed of farmers who fenced their fields and used the plow as whites did. "Civilized" people were Christians who knew how to read and write the English language. They lived in houses like those of whites, ate meals at regular times, had proper table manners, dressed appropriately, and otherwise behaved like whites. "Civilized" people also governed themselves by written law, not custom, under a republican government like that of the United States. This very narrow view of human society had no appreciation for the cultural differences between non-Indians and Native Americans. Nevertheless, this view rested on the assumption that although Indian *cultures* were inferior and doomed, Indian *people* were equal to Europeans. Cultural transformation promised them survival and, ultimately, assimilation.

The U.S. government sent agents to live with the Cherokees and other Native peoples. The most successful agent to the Cherokees was Return J. Meigs, who lived among the

Cherokees from 1801 to 1823. Meigs established a farm modeled after those of white Americans and instructed the Cherokees in "civilized" life. He distributed plows to men and spinning wheels and looms to women. He hired blacksmiths and millers to set up shop in Cherokee country. Meigs and other agents also supervised trade between whites and Indians, and they sought to enforce laws against the sale of liquor, the consumption of which they regarded as harmful to Indian society.

Meigs, like other Indian agents, believed that the continuation of the deerskin trade with the Cherokees was detrimental to their "civilization" because it encouraged hunting rather than farming as a livelihood. For that reason, Meigs persuaded the Cherokees to cede their hunting grounds to the United States. In giving up this land, the Indians would by necessity give up hunting and would also clear the way for white pioneers. Thus, Meigs aided white expansion into Cherokee territory and sometimes seemed to be working in the service of whites rather than Indians.

The United States also encouraged and supported missionary work among the Cherokees. Agents and missionaries both believed that "civilization" and Christianity were inseparable: A person could not be a Christian without being "civilized," nor "civilized" without being Christian. The American government helped fund missions, and the missionaries instructed the Cherokees in farming and cooking, and taught them about the Bible.

Although there had been some missionaries among the Cherokees in the late 1700s, it was not until the next century that Protestant missionaries of German origin called Moravians established the first permanent mission outpost in the Cherokees' homeland. In 1800, the Moravians obtained the consent of a Cherokee council to open a school. The Cherokees were not interested in Christianity, but they were anxious for their children to learn to read and write English. The Moravians built their mission at Spring Place in present-day North Georgia. When they seemed more interested in converting the Cherokees than in teaching their children, the Cherokee council threatened to banish them, so they began their efforts at education in earnest. In fact, the Moravians found that most Cherokees were happy with their own religion: They won their first Cherokee convert to Christianity nine years after they had opened their mission.

Except for an ill-fated Presbyterian mission, the Moravians labored alone in the Cherokee Nation until 1817, when the American Board of Commissioners for Foreign Missions opened a missionary station just east of present-day Chattanooga, Tennessee. The American Board was an interdenominational mission effort composed primarily of northern Presbyterians and Congregationalists and headquartered in Boston. One of the American Board's own missionaries criticized his colleagues for preferring to minister to wealthy, highly *acculturated* Cherokees with whom they felt socially comfortable. Association with prominent Cherokees, however, placed American Board missionaries in positions in which they had considerable influence. They helped the Cherokees procure a printing press, for example, and they marshaled opposition to removal among New Englanders.

Baptists and Methodists soon joined the American Board, and these two denominations tended to appeal to less affluent Cherokees. At the Baptist mission in western North Carolina, missionary Evan Jones ministered to a particularly conservative Cherokee community. Unlike most American Board missionaries, Jones learned to speak Cherokee and came to tolerate traditional Cherokee customs as long as they did not directly conflict with Christian teachings. He also actively recruited and ordained Cherokee ministers.

The Methodists ministered to the Cherokees with traveling missionaries (also called circuit riders) who preached in open-air camp meetings and in Sunday schools. Unlike the

Moravians, they did not establish permanent outposts to perform their work among the Indians. Nor did they have boarding schools. Instead, Methodists taught children and adults the rudiments of reading and writing on Sunday afternoons after services. The other denominations criticized the Methodists for this approach because they believed that the Indians needed intensive training and constant supervision to prevent them from lapsing back into their "savage" ways.

The majority of missionaries focused their efforts on the youngest members of Cherokee society. They thought that most adult Cherokees were too set in their ways to change dramatically. They had high hopes, however, for the children, particularly if they could be removed from the "harmful" influence of their parents and educated in boarding schools. The children who attended these boarding schools only occasionally visited their parents, and thus many of them gradually began to lose contact with their traditional culture. They accepted the missionaries' view of what was appropriate behavior and gradually came to regard their parents as "unenlightened."

In these boarding schools, the children learned the English language and studied arithmetic, geography, and other subjects. They read the Bible, prayed, and attended church services regularly. The boys plowed, built fences, chopped wood, planted and harvested crops, and performed other tasks that missionaries thought were suitable for boys. Girls no longer worked in fields as their ancestors had; now they cooked, cleaned, ironed, sewed, and did other domestic chores deemed appropriate for young ladies.

Missionary societies, primarily in New England, supported children in mission schools by sending them clothing and books. They also paid for the right to rename Cherokee children who enrolled in school. As a first step toward "civilization," Cherokee children surrendered their Indian names in exchange for names like John Huss, David Brainerd, or other names that missionary societies requested. Children often corresponded with their benefactors. Nancy Reece, a student at Brainerd, an American Board school in Tennessee for Indian children, wrote a New England minister about her school in 1828:

> I will tell you something of our happy school, so you may know how we shall feel if we should be separated from each other, and from our teachers and other missionaries. Miss Ames has twenty-nine scholars; one more is expected which will make the school full. The studies in our school are Reading, Spelling, Writing, Geography, Arithmetick; two have begun to study grammar. Eight new scholars have entered school this year. Part of them cannot talk English, and Miss Ames is obliged to have me interpret for her. . . . When school hours are over, the girls attend to domestic concerns and learn to make their own clothes and the clothes of the boys so they can do such work when they go home, to assist their parents. They can then take care of their houses and their brothers and sisters and perhaps can learn their parents something that they do not understand. . . . The boys chop wood and in summer help about the farm and some that have left school are learning the blacksmith's trade.

Nancy Reece also wrote that she and her friends spent some of their spare time imitating New England missionary societies: They sewed bonnets and other items and then sold them to neighboring Cherokees. They sent the money to the American Board for the use of "the heathen who have not had missionaries as we have."

The children in mission schools did not always behave in ways that earned them the missionaries' approval. Cherokee children were very uninhibited: Boys and girls swam together without clothing and played games together wearing little more. They talked openly about sex and made off-color jokes to each other. Missionaries also found them vain and complained that they loved the pretty clothes and ornaments that the teachers thought were frivolous. The missionaries, however, had to use care in punishing children. Cherokee parents rarely disciplined their children and never used corporal punishment. If they discovered that a missionary had spanked a child, they often withdrew the child from school. Therefore, the missionaries resorted to another form of punishment: They required students to memorize Bible verses appropriate to their infractions.

Missionaries and agents were remarkably successful in transforming the Cherokees' culture but only because many Cherokees had decided that these changes were in their own best interest. Parents sent their children to school, even with the understanding that they might become estranged from them, because they wanted their children to be able to deal more effectively with whites. In time, many adult Cherokees began to adopt new ways. Women learned to spin and weave, while men opened stores and operated ferries and toll roads. At the same time, "civilization" gave Cherokees new ideas, like nationalism, and new strategies to resist growing pressure for their land.

The Cherokee Nation officially adopted the "civilization" program of the U.S. government because Cherokee leaders believed that if their people were culturally indistinguishable from whites, the white people would permit them to live in peace in their homeland. The Cherokee government supported the work of the missionaries and sought to further the educational opportunities of its citizens. With the help of missionaries, the Nation managed to buy a printing press and typefaces in both English and in the alphabet invented by the Cherokee Sequoyah.

Sequoyah had been born about 1770. He had a traditional Cherokee childhood and never learned English. He did recognize, however, the tremendous advantage English speakers enjoyed by being able to write their language. He wanted his own people to have that advantage. About 1809, he began

Sequoyah (c. 1770–1843) is perhaps the most famous Cherokee. He is known to people throughout the world as the creator of the Cherokee syllabary—the system that allowed the Cherokee Nation to have a written language for the first time in its history.

work on a Cherokee alphabet. Sequoyah struggled for more than a decade. Finally, he arrived at a system that worked, and within months, he had developed eighty-six symbols (later reduced to eighty-five) that stood for Cherokee syllables.

Because Sequoyah knew no alphabet, he invented his own symbols for Cherokee. Some of these symbols resemble those from the alphabet in which English is written; some appear to be adapted from the Greek alphabet, which Sequoyah may have seen at a mission station; others seem to have been created by him. Whatever their origins, the symbols of the Sequoyah syllabary, as a writing system based on syllables is called, provided an efficient way to write the Cherokee language. The Cherokees enthusiastically adopted Sequoyah's syllabary and soon used it in place of a rival writing system developed by white missionaries. The system was remarkably easy to learn: Anyone who spoke Cherokee fluently could reportedly read and write the language in a few days. The Cherokees quickly became a literate people.

In 1828, the *Cherokee Phoenix*, a bilingual newspaper, began publication under the editorship of Elias Boudinot, a young Cherokee man who had been educated in mission schools in the Cherokee Nation and in New England. In columns of alternating Cherokee and English, Boudinot printed the laws of the Nation, local news, world news, human interest stories, Bible passages, editorials, and advertisements. Subscribers to the paper included not only Cherokees but interested whites in the United States and Europe. (For additional information on the United States' first Native American newspaper, enter "The Cherokee Phoenix" into any search engine and browse the many sites listed.)

The *Cherokee Phoenix*, the Sequoyah syllabary, and the mission schools pointed to the success of the "civilization" program. Another outgrowth of the program was the development of commercial agriculture among the Cherokees. Because they held the title (or legal ownership) to their country in common, the Cherokees did not need to buy land, and, therefore, they could farm as much land as they wished as long as they did not infringe on acreage that had already been claimed. The Cherokees who accumulated money through business ventures other than farming could invest their earnings in improvements on their property.

Some prosperous Cherokees bought African slaves to work their fields and expanded their farms into plantations. The

Ꭰ	a	Ꭶ	ga	Ꭷ	ka	Ꭽ	ha
Ꮃ	la	Ꮉ	ma	Ꮎ	na	Ꮏ	hna
Ꮐ	nah	Ꮖ	qua	Ꮜ	sa	Ꮝ	s
Ꮣ	da	Ꮤ	ta	Ꮬ	dla	Ꮭ	tla
Ꮳ	tsa	Ꮹ	wa	Ꮿ	ya	Ꭱ	e
Ꭸ	ge	Ꭾ	he	Ꮄ	le	Ꮊ	me
Ꮑ	ne	Ꮗ	que	Ꮞ	se	Ꮥ	de
Ꮦ	te	Ꮮ	tle	Ꮴ	tse	Ꮺ	we
Ᏸ	ye	Ꭲ	i	Ꭹ	gi	Ꭿ	hi
Ꮅ	li	Ꮋ	mi	Ꮒ	ni	Ꮘ	qui
Ꮟ	si	Ꮧ	di	Ꮨ	ti	Ꮯ	tli
Ꮵ	tsi	Ꮻ	wi	Ᏹ	yi	Ꭳ	o
Ꭺ	go	Ꮀ	ho	Ꮆ	lo	Ꮌ	mo
Ꮓ	no	Ꮙ	quo	Ꮠ	so	Ꮩ	do
Ꮰ	tlo	Ꮶ	tso	Ꮼ	wo	Ᏺ	yo
Ꭴ	u	Ꭻ	gu	Ꮁ	hu	Ꮇ	lu
Ꮍ	mu	Ꮔ	nu	Ꮚ	quu	Ꮡ	su
Ꮪ	du	Ꮱ	tlu	Ꮷ	tsu	Ꮽ	wu
Ᏻ	yu	Ꭵ	v	Ꭼ	gv	Ꮂ	hv
Ꮈ	lv	Ꮕ	nv	Ꮛ	quv		
Ꮢ	sv	Ꮫ	dv	Ꮲ	tlv		
Ꮸ	tsv	Ꮾ	wv	Ᏼ	yv		

The Cherokee syllabary is composed of eighty-five syllables—some of which resemble letters from both the English and Greek alphabets. The syllabary helped thousands of Cherokees to learn how to read and write and gave them the impetus to publish the United States' first Native American newspaper, the *Cherokee Phoenix*, in 1828.

purchase of slaves conformed to the United States' civilization program, but the practice also provided Cherokee men with a way to avoid farming, which traditionally was viewed as women's work. Some Cherokee planters built elegant houses that they embellished with imported furniture, china, and other luxury items. They added to their wealth by operating stores, mills, ferries, taverns, and toll roads. These men were wealthy by anyone's standards.

Among these Cherokee planters were the brothers John and Lewis Ross. Descendants of white traders and Cherokee women, the Rosses owned several stores and plantations. John Ross, who was principal chief of the Cherokees from 1828 until his death in 1866, lived in a two-story weatherboard house with four fireplaces and twenty glass windows, extravagant fixtures for the time.

Ross' plantation at the head of the Coosa River in present-day North Georgia included workshops, smokehouses, stables, corncribs, a blacksmith shop, a wagon house, and slave quarters. By 1835, Ross owned nineteen slaves. He grew corn, wheat, and cotton and had peach and apple orchards. He also operated a ferry on the Coosa River and made a profit of about $1,000 per year.

John's brother Lewis owned several stores, a mill, three ferryboats, and more than forty slaves. He lived in what visiting New Englanders described as "an elegant white house near the bank of the river, as neatly furnished as almost any in Litchfield County [with] Negroes enough to wait on us."

Perhaps the wealthiest man in the Cherokee Nation was John Ross' friend Joseph Vann, who lived in a magnificent red brick mansion at Spring Place in North Georgia. In 1835, he owned 110 slaves who cultivated 300 acres, and he operated a mill, ferry, and tavern.

The accumulation of individual property led many Cherokees to believe that they needed a more formal legal system in order to protect their holdings. In 1808, a council of delegates from the major towns met, and in the first written Cherokee law, they established a national police force, called the Lighthorse Guard, to protect property. The law removed a major function of Cherokee clans, which was to offer protection to members, and shifted the responsibility to the Cherokee national government. The law also guaranteed that the wife and children would inherit a man's possessions after he died, whereas Cherokee custom had previously dictated that a man's property go to his sister and her children. A later law reaffirmed this traditional practice as well, revealing cultural diversity within Cherokee society and some resistance to change.

As the Cherokees formalized their judicial code, they also reorganized their method of governing. Cherokee town councils were no longer acting independently and instead joined together to create a true national government that rendered the traditional town councils obsolete. Although they might still resolve local disputes, councils no longer wielded the power they once had. Most Cherokees, even those who were not wealthy, supported this change. They believed that a strong central government would be best able to protect the land that all Cherokees held in common. A central government that could be held accountable to Cherokee voters would be less likely to succumb to pressure and bribes from whites who were trying to obtain Cherokee land. In 1817, the Cherokees divided their nation into eight electoral districts, each of which sent representatives to the national council. As government shifted from clans and towns to a representative and elected national council, women became formally disenfranchised, although they continued to exercise considerable influence on Cherokee politics.

The Cherokees not only empowered their national government to protect personal and common property, but they also gave the government judicial power—the right to determine guilt and innocence in criminal cases. The fate of criminals had previously been determined by clans within each village, but in

1810, representatives of the seven clans renounced blood vengeance under limited circumstances, which began the process of shifting judicial power to the emerging national government. District courts eventually tried criminal cases, and in 1822, the Cherokees established a supreme court to hear appeals from the district courts.

The culmination of this trend toward centralization and formalization of political power came in 1827 when the Cherokees wrote a constitution modeled after that of the United States:

> WE, THE REPRESENTATIVES of the people of the CHEROKEE NATION in Convention assembled, in order to establish justice, ensure tranquility, promote the common welfare, and secure to ourselves and our posterity the blessing of liberty: acknowledging with humility and gratitude the goodness of the sovereign Ruler of the Universe, in offering us an opportunity so favorable to the design, and imploring his aid and direction in its accomplishment, do ordain and establish this Constitution for the Government of the Cherokee Nation.

The constitution provided for the General Council, a legislature composed of two houses: the National Council, a body of thirty-two members, and the thirteen-member National Committee. The Cherokees directly elected members of both houses. The General Council, in turn, chose the executive branch of the government, which consisted of the principal chief, the vice-principal chief, and the treasurer of the Cherokee Nation. The judicial branch, established by earlier legislation, continued to assume responsibility for weighing guilt and meting out punishments for crimes. Neither women nor people of African descent could vote under this document.

Unlike the Constitution of the United States, the Cherokee Constitution defined the geographical boundaries of the Cherokee Nation. In this way, the Cherokees indicated that they had no intention of expanding and, more importantly, that they intended to remain in their homeland. The constitution also affirmed that Cherokee land belonged to the nation and not to individuals. An individual, therefore, could not simply sell his land and move west. Only the nation could sell land and this it would not do.

The writing of a republican constitution, the establishment of mission schools, the development of commercial agriculture, and the invention and adoption of Sequoyah's syllabary reflect profound changes that forever altered the fabric of Cherokee life. This transformation should not be interpreted simply as the destruction of traditional Cherokee society. Even in the face of intense pressure from whites, Cherokees maintained control over the evolution of their culture. Although the Cherokees adopted schools, churches, and political institutions from Anglo-Americans, they used them to serve their own purposes. In some respects, the "civilization" of the Cherokees was really cultural revitalization that produced an intense pride in being Cherokee and a sense of Cherokee nationalism previously unknown in the history of the principal people.

4

Removal

The creation of the Cherokee republic in 1827 precipitated a crisis for the U.S. government. The territory that the constitution explicitly delineated as belonging to the Cherokee Nation was claimed by four states—Georgia, Alabama, Tennessee, and North Carolina. The United States insisted that a Cherokee republic was illegal because it violated state sovereignty, as set forth by the U.S. Constitution in Article IV, Section 3: ". . . no new State shall be formed or erected within the jurisdiction of any other State . . ." In formally asserting their right to their tribal lands, the Cherokees had created a state within a state, a violation of federal law. Thus, the United States gave the state governments an opportunity to challenge the Indians' right to the land and to promote the removal of all Indians to territory west of the Mississippi River, thereby opening the Indian land to white settlers.

Relations between Cherokees and the U.S. government had long suffered from disputes over land, despite decades of treaties and negotiations. The states' claim to Cherokee land rested on the precedent established by Europeans when they first arrived in the Americas in the sixteenth century. In fact, the American attitude toward the principal people can be traced directly to the views of the earliest European explorers to the New World, who had posed the question, "Who owns the land?" Because they wanted the land and all the riches it promised, Europeans were reluctant to admit that Native Americans had legitimate claim to the territory they had occupied for centuries. The Indians had no absolute right of ownership, Europeans insisted, because they were not Christians and because they had not put the land to its "proper use." Therefore, the European nations argued, the Indians had only the right to occupy the land, but its ultimate ownership rested with the European countries that had discovered it.

During the seventeenth century, English colonists in North America agreed to purchase occupancy rights from Native Americans if the latter agreed to vacate their territory. The treaties governing these deals usually called for the Cherokees and other tribes to turn over valuable holdings for a pittance. Tribal leaders signed away thousands of acres to the British without understanding that they were, in effect, being robbed of their land under the guise of international law.

After the American Revolution, the United States inherited English claims to Indian land and also adopted British methods of negotiating with the Indians. The new republic forced the Cherokees into a series of punitive treaties—retaliation for some of the alliances Indians had forged with the British during the War of Independence—that ceded large portions of the Cherokee homeland to the U.S. government. No sooner had they claimed this new turf than the Americans set their sights on an even greater share of Indian land, but they knew they must win it without a costly war.

At first, it seemed that the Cherokees might oblige the United States and move out of the way. In the late eighteenth century, many Cherokees who opposed peaceful relations with the United States moved west into present-day Arkansas and Texas. Other Cherokees who wanted to pursue a life focused on hunting joined them. Cherokees from the East sometimes visited their western brothers to hunt game, which had become scarce in the East, or to make war on the Osage, their traditional enemies.

Not all Cherokees who preferred a traditional way of life, however, went west. Many remained in the East, where they made their views in opposition to the "civilization" program known. They insisted that the council honor matrilineal as well as patrilineal descent and protect the rights of married women to own property apart from their husbands. Both of these measures were counter to laws in the United States, which the "civilization" program urged Cherokees to emulate. Some Cherokees objected to the presence of missionaries, who discouraged converts from playing stickball, engaging in dances, and practicing traditional medicine. A group under the leadership of White Path briefly threatened rebellion when the Cherokee council called the Constitutional Convention in 1827 but open resistance soon dissipated. The persistence of traditional culture troubled acculturated leaders such as Principal Chief John Ross and *Cherokee Phoenix* editor Elias Boudinot. Missionaries and U.S. agents also found this traditionalism disturbing.

Some Cherokees' rejection of the "civilization" program seemed to confirm what many Americans were beginning to believe about Indians—that they were primitive peoples whose behavior would always be dictated by their inferior racial traits. Whites who wanted Cherokee land unjustly charged that most Cherokees were still "savages" and that Cherokee leaders concealed this "savagery" in order to protect their own power and property. These whites demanded that the Cherokees and other Indians be removed from "civilized" society.

John Ross was elected principal chief of the Cherokees in 1828 and served in that capacity until his death in 1866. Despite his efforts to organize the Cherokee tribe as a nation, with its own constitution, the U.S. government forced them to move west to Oklahoma in 1838.

Where, then, were the Cherokees to go? President Thomas Jefferson had provided an answer: "Uncivilized" Indians could go west of the Mississippi River to land that had been acquired by the United States in 1803 as part of the Louisiana Purchase. This territory extended from the Mississippi River to the Rocky Mountains and from the Gulf of Mexico to what is now Canada. The purchase of this vast area doubled the size of the

United States. No one could imagine a day when the United States would need this land for its white citizens, so sending the Indians there seemed to be a permanent solution.

Jefferson suggested that the eastern Indians who wished to follow a more traditional lifestyle could move to this wilderness. He ignored the other Indian nations who already claimed this territory as their homeland. After Congress had confirmed the Louisiana Purchase, it had also authorized the president to negotiate exchanges of land and the removal of eastern Indians to the West. Exchanges were, of course, supposed to be entirely voluntary. Jefferson believed that only the most culturally conservative Indians would go west, where they could acclimate to "civilization" at their own pace. All those who remained in the East would quickly be assimilated into white society and their separate nations would disappear.

Jefferson's efforts to convince eastern Indians to move west created a crisis for the Cherokees in 1808. At this time, the Cherokees were not yet a centralized nation. Although a national council composed of representatives from traditional towns met annually and a principal chief spoke for the Cherokee Nation, serious disagreements existed between two regions. The lower towns in Alabama and Georgia were much more committed to "civilization" and to assimilation than the upper towns of western North Carolina and eastern Tennessee.

Contrary to Jefferson's expectations, leaders of the lower towns favored an exchange of territory and persuaded Principal Chief Black Fox to support them. The opponents of the removal deposed Black Fox and made one of their number, Path Killer, principal chief instead. The actions of lower town chiefs did not even reflect the wishes of the Cherokees in their region who, like a majority of Cherokees across the homeland, opposed removal to the West. The U.S. government knew that most Cherokees wanted to prevent the exchange of eastern for western land but it persisted in its efforts to relocate the Indians. Unable to obtain a treaty from the national council,

U.S. commissioners finally got an agreement from lower town chiefs. These leaders signed a treaty and then departed for their new homes in what is now Arkansas, accompanied by their followers.

Another major Cherokee land cession and emigration took place in 1817–1819. Once again, U.S. treaty commissioners negotiated with minority chiefs and virtually bribed them into signing a treaty. For those who elected to go west under the treaties of 1817 and 1819, the U.S. government agreed to pay wealthy Cherokees the full value of their improvements—that is, their houses, barns, fences, and orchards. Poor Indians were promised "a rifle, ammunition, blanket, and brass kettle or beaver trap each, as full compensation." The United States also pledged to pay the cost of their removal to the West.

The new agreement mirrored the 1810 treaty in its promise of land "exchange" but differed from it in a unique clause known as the "reservation clause." U.S. commissioners offered Cherokees who lived within the ceded territory an opportunity to remain on their land. Anyone who chose to become a U.S. citizen could receive a reservation of 640 acres. A *reservation* was a privately owned tract of land within ceded territory. An Indian receiving such a reservation could do whatever he wished with it within the limits of U.S. law: He could sell it, lease it, or live on it.

About 150 Cherokees took advantage of this provision. Some wanted the land for speculation; that is, they planned to hold it until land values went up and then sell it for a profit. Other Cherokees, however, wanted to live on their reservations and become U.S. citizens, but a number of problems arose that eventually forced most of these people to return to the Cherokee Nation. Some had reservations located on land that the United States had already granted to veterans of the War of 1812. Others had reservations occupied by squatters, who refused to move. Finally, increasingly harsh racial attitudes and state laws discriminated against Indians as "people of color."

Holders of reservations preferred equality in the Cherokee Nation to second-class status in the United States.

The land exchanges of both 1810 and 1817–1819 held surprising consequences for both Jefferson and later proponents of removal. They had hoped that Cherokee traditionalists, people who wanted to preserve the old way of life, would go west while people who had adopted Anglo-American culture would become assimilated. A few Cherokees who moved west were indeed traditionalists, but a surprisingly large number fell into the group who had embraced the "civilization" program. Some went west to escape political enemies who held treaty signers responsible for the loss of land in the East. Some no doubt sought to distance themselves from the increasingly racist Anglo-American society that refused to acknowledge their accomplishments. Still others, like many white pioneers, may have gone west in search of greater economic opportunities.

Most Cherokee traditionalists, however, refused to move west. The Cherokees, traditionalists believed, lived in the center of the world. Why should they move to the edge of the earth, which they believed was an island? Traditionalists had a long list of objections to moving west: They thought that the spirits of the dead lived there; they viewed the mountains and valleys of their homeland as a holy place; and they feared that the native plants from which they made sacred medicines used to cure physical and spiritual ills did not grow in the West.

Another unforeseen consequence of these early removals was the waning enthusiasm for westward migration among those Cherokees who remained in the East. U.S. government officials had hoped that the trickle of emigrants would swell to a stream. Instead, those Indians who wanted to go west simply went, thereby relieving eastern Cherokees of a pro-removal faction. These removals also deprived U.S. negotiators of individuals who might be inclined to sign another removal treaty.

Opposition to removal, in fact, increased among Cherokees who remained in the East. One reason the Cherokees formalized their political system, recorded their laws, and wrote their constitution was to protect their homeland. The National Council served notice to the United States in 1819 that the Cherokees would cede no more land. The council also soon enacted a law that reaffirmed and committed to writing an earlier understanding that any Cherokee who signed a treaty selling land would be executed.

Cherokee resolve to remain in the East strengthened at the very time that white Southerners became more determined that the Indians should go west. Cotton quickly was becoming king in the South, and the Indians occupied land that was suitable for cotton growing. Southern states demanded that the federal government, which controlled Indian relations, expel the Indians. Georgia, the cotton state with the largest Cherokee population, insisted that the federal government live up to the terms of the Compact of 1802.

In this agreement, the state gave up territory, which eventually became Alabama and Mississippi, on the condition that the federal government extinguish Indian title to land within the state. Most people believed that this could be done easily through treaties, and until 1819, the federal government had been making some progress with the Cherokees. But their refusal to make any further cessions meant the federal government could not fulfill the Compact of 1802. Georgians were furious. The discovery of gold in the Cherokee country at about the same time no doubt contributed to the Georgians' indignation.

The Cherokees' establishment of a republican government with a written constitution in 1827 gave Georgia an opportunity to press its claim to Cherokee land by accusing the principal people of violating state sovereignty. In order to reaffirm state power over territory within the Cherokee Nation, the Georgia legislature abolished the Cherokee government and prohibited the council from meeting. The state legislature extended Georgia law to include the Cherokees, passed a series of discriminatory acts that forbade the Cherokees from mining their own gold, from using their own court system, and from testifying against whites in Georgia courts. The state then created a special police force, the Georgia Guard, to enforce these laws among the Cherokees. The legislature clearly wanted to make life so miserable for the Cherokees that they would leave. The legislators also authorized a survey and distribution of Cherokee lands to whites in a lottery.

During this time, the Cherokees received little help from the federal government, least of all from the executive office, occupied by President Andrew Jackson from 1829 to 1837. Jackson had achieved fame as an Indian fighter, and he had negotiated several questionable treaties with the Cherokees and neighboring Indians. The president was determined to acquire Cherokee land and open it to white settlement. He offered the Cherokees a choice: They could accept the discriminatory laws of the states or they could move west. He, of course, believed that they should move. In 1830, Congress passed the *Indian Removal Act*, which authorized the president to negotiate with the Indians and appropriated $500,000 for that purpose. The Cherokees, fearing that the appropriation would be used for bribes, were distressed by the congressional action, but they also were determined to resist. (For additional information on this act, enter "Indian Removal Act" into any search engine and browse the many sites listed.)

The suffering experienced by the Creeks, Choctaws, and Chickasaws, other Indians who *did* negotiate removal treaties, strengthened the Cherokees' resolve to remain in their home-land. They turned to the U.S. courts for justice. In 1831, the U.S. Supreme Court ruled in *Cherokee Nation* v. *Georgia* that the Cherokee Nation was a "domestic dependent nation" and had no standing before the court. Refusing to give up, the

Andrew Jackson served as U.S. president from 1829 to 1837. A former soldier and Indian fighter, he was particularly devoted to removing the Native Americans of the East to lands west of the Mississippi River. In fact, he instituted the removal policy that eventually forced the Cherokees to undergo the terrible forced march, or Trail of Tears, during the winter of 1838–1839.

Cherokees hoped for a more conclusive and beneficial ruling the next year in *Worcester* v. *Georgia*.

Samuel A. Worcester was a white missionary to the Cherokees. The Georgia Guard arrested him and another missionary for violating the state law that required all whites living in the Cherokee Nation to take an oath of allegiance to the state. Because Worcester was a citizen of the United States, he clearly had standing before U.S. courts of law. In this case, the Cherokees triumphed. The Court ruled that Georgia law did not extend over the Cherokees and ordered the state to release the missionaries. The Cherokee victory, however, was short-lived. The Georgia government ignored the ruling of the Supreme Court. Legal technicalities coupled with an unwillingness to help the Cherokees kept Jackson from enforcing the decision. The missionaries remained in prison and Georgians continued to harass the Cherokees.

When it became obvious that the Supreme Court decision would have little impact on the situation in the Cherokee Nation, a small group of Cherokees began to consider negotiating removal. Known as the Treaty Party, this group's leaders included Major Ridge—who had fought with the United States in the War of 1812—his mission-educated son John, and his nephew Elias Boudinot, the editor of the *Cherokee Phoenix*. Motivated at least as much by economic and political ambitions as by concern for the Cherokee people, the Treaty Party enjoyed little support within the Cherokee Nation.

The vast majority of Cherokees supported Principal Chief John Ross in his steadfast opposition to removal. Nevertheless, U.S. treaty commissioners met with about a hundred Treaty Party members in December 1835, and they negotiated the Treaty of New Echota. This treaty provided for the exchange of all Cherokee territory in the Southeast for a tract of land in what is today northeastern Oklahoma.

Fifteen thousand Cherokees, almost the entire population, signed a petition protesting this treaty, which had been negotiated by an unauthorized minority. Nevertheless, the U.S. Senate ratified the document. The treaty gave the Cherokees two years to go west. Confident that justice would ultimately triumph, the Cherokees made no preparations to move. Finally, in the summer of 1838, federal troops entered the Cherokee Nation

When the Cherokees were removed from their eastern lands, violence erupted between those who had previously elected to move west and those who had been forced to move in 1838–1839. Just when the two sides appeared to reach a settlement, John Ridge (pictured here) and two other leaders of the Treaty Party (his father and cousin) were killed.

and began rounding up the Cherokees and imprisoning them in stockades. The soldiers often burned the captives' cabins and crops in order to discourage them from escaping and returning home. In the soldiers' sweep of Indian villages, parents and children often became separated.

Once they reached the stockades, the Cherokees did not have enough food, water, or shelter. The transport of approximately three thousand Cherokees in the summer of 1838 was fraught with difficulties. Chief Ross and other Cherokee leaders

The Trail of Tears,
as Seen through the Eyes of a White Man

John G. Burnett was a U.S. Army private during the winter of 1838–1839. Born in Tennessee, he spent many days in his youth hunting in the hills and forests of the Cherokee Nation and came to know them well. He felt a deep attachment to the Cherokees, despite his eventual induction into the army and his participation in the removal of the Cherokees from their homeland. In 1890, nearly fifty years after the Cherokees had trekked from Georgia to Oklahoma, Burnett recorded his account of the Trail of Tears.

> The removal of the Cherokee Indians from their life long homes in the year of 1838 found me a young man in the prime of life and a Private . . . in the American Army. Being acquainted with many of the Indians and able to fluently speak their language, I was sent as interpreter into the Smokey Mountain Country [where I] witnessed the execution of the most brutal order in the history of American warfare. I saw the helpless Cherokees arrested and dragged from their homes, and driven at the bayonet point into the stockades. And in the chill of a drizzling rain on an October morning I saw them loaded like cattle or sheep into six hundred and forty-five wagons and started toward the west. . . .

> The trail of the exiles was a trail of death. They had to sleep in the wagons and on the ground without fire. I have known as many as 22 of them to die in one night of pneumonia due to ill treatment, cold and exposure. Among this number was the beautiful Christian wife of Chief John Ross. This noble hearted woman died a martyr to childhood, giving her only blanket for the protection of a sick child. She rode thinly clad through a blinding sleet and snow storm, developed pneumonia and died in the still hours of a bleak winter night. . . .

> The long painful journey to the west ended March 26, 1839, with four thousand silent graves reaching from the foothills of the Smokey Mountains to what is known as the Indian Territory in the West. And the covetousness on the part of the white race was the cause of all that the Cherokees had to suffer.

Source: Full text available online at *http://www.cherokee.org/culture/HistoryPage.asp?ID=49*

appealed to President Martin Van Buren, Jackson's successor in the White House, to permit the Cherokees to conduct their own removal to the West. Van Buren consented, and in the winter of 1838–1839, the Cherokee Nation moved west. This forced migration came to be known as the *Trail of Tears* because of the Cherokees' suffering. Between one-fourth and one-half of them died before reaching their new home in the West.

Cherokee removal ranks as one of the greatest tragedies in American history. The Cherokees, more than any other Native people, tried to comply with the U.S. "civilization" program. They had become literate, Christian farmers governed by republican laws. Yet, in the end, none of that mattered as much as the determination of whites to clear the southeastern United States of Indians.

5

The Cherokees in the West

In the spring of 1839, the Cherokees who survived the Trail of Tears joined two other branches of the principal people in the West: the Treaty Party and the Old Settlers. Most members of the Treaty Party, fearing reprisals from their countrymen, had left the Cherokee Nation in the East promptly after signing the Treaty of New Echota in 1835. They traveled to what is today northeastern Oklahoma, where the western Cherokees, known as the Old Settlers, lived. In the first decade of the nineteenth century, the Old Settlers moved from the East to Arkansas, which, like Oklahoma, was part of Jefferson's Louisiana Purchase. They had intended to settle there permanently, but within twenty years, white frontiersmen demanded their removal. In 1828, they moved farther west, taking their customs and institutions with them.

The Old Settlers, the Treaty Party, and the National Party—as those who had opposed removal were known—now occupied the same territory but the differences among them produced considerable conflict in the new Cherokee Nation in the West. For example, Old Settler Cherokees resented the newcomers, particularly the National Party, who greatly outnumbered them. The Old Settlers were understandably apprehensive about the influx of thousands of Cherokees because the former had their own laws and chiefs, and they did not want to come under the rule of the far more numerous newcomers.

A more severe conflict divided the members of the Treaty Party and the National Party. These groups bore great enmity for one another because in the East they had clashed over the issue of removal. Because they went west before their eastern adversaries, members of the Treaty Party had an opportunity to forge an alliance with the Old Settlers prior to the arrival of Chief John Ross and the majority of Cherokees. The Old Settlers found allies among the Treaty Party, whose members certainly did not want to become subject to the rule of people who regarded them as traitors. Therefore, when the main body of Cherokees from the East arrived they found an alliance of the Treaty Party and Old Settlers who opposed the establishment of the eastern Cherokee Nation's institutions, laws, and leaders in the West—which was exactly the course of action that Principal Chief John Ross and his followers had in mind.

The National Party and the Old Settlers formally met in June 1839, but they reached no new accord. The Old Settlers could not understand why the eastern Cherokees refused to accept the government they found in the West, as had the members of the Treaty Party. Plans were made for another meeting of the Old Settlers and the eastern Cherokees, and there was hope that the two groups could resolve their problems.

Before the second meeting could take place, chaos erupted among the Cherokees. At dawn on June 22, 1839, a group of armed men dragged John Ridge from his bed and into the yard, where they stabbed him to death as his family looked on in horror. Later in the morning, his father, Major Ridge, was shot from his horse. At about the same time, several men asked Elias Boudinot for medicine that he normally dispensed from a nearby mission. On the way to the mission, they stabbed him repeatedly. Others, too, were slated for execution—among them Boudinot's brother, Stand Watie—but managed to escape.

Watie immediately gathered armed men around him to protect himself and to avenge his kinsmen's deaths. A likely target of Watie's wrath was John Ross, who apparently knew nothing of the plan to execute prominent members of the Treaty Party, but whom Watie and others held responsible for the attacks. An armed guard assembled to protect Chief Ross. Then, a council dominated by Ross' supporters quickly voted to pardon those who had killed the three treaty signers and offered amnesty to members of the Treaty Party. Because the amnesty agreement excluded those who accepted it from participation in Cherokee government, Watie and most other Treaty Party members declined the offer.

Many Old Settlers realized that civil war threatened, and so they moved to unify the Nation. Several of their leaders joined with Ross' followers on September 6, 1839, in drafting a new constitution that closely resembled the one written in 1827 in the East. Under this constitution, Ross was elected principal chief but Old Settlers occupied other important offices. Some Old Settlers, however, refused to recognize Ross' leadership and the government established under the Constitution of 1839.

U.S. officials aggravated the situation by continuing to recognize three distinct groups of Cherokees—the Old Settlers, the Treaty Party, and the National Party—although a majority of Cherokees supported the Constitution of 1839.

In opposition to Principal Chief John Ross and the majority of Cherokees, Stand Watie (pictured here) and members of the Treaty Party signed the Treaty of New Echota in 1835. The treaty provided for removal of the Cherokees to the West, and as a result, a seven-year civil war erupted between the two sides.

The Office of Indian Affairs, established in 1824, accepted delegations from various factions and the U.S. agent to the Cherokees gave all of them a hearing. This encouraged the

Old Settlers and the Treaty Party to oppose a resolution to the discord, particularly one that would confer a minority status on them.

For seven years, intermittent war raged among the Cherokees. Some of those who rebelled against a unified nation, such as Stand Watie and other signers of the New Echota treaty, also sought to avenge the deaths of kinsmen, thereby increasing the bloodshed. Some Cherokees became little more than outlaws. For example, Tom Starr and his brothers claimed to want only to protect the life of their father (who opposed the new national government) but murder and robbery soon became a way of life for them. They terrorized the Cherokee Nation until 1848, when the leaders of the gang were killed.

The civil war finally came to an end in 1846 when Ross, Watie, and other Cherokee leaders agreed to a treaty. The treaty pardoned all Cherokees who had committed crimes and created a united Cherokee Nation. The treaty did not mean that all past conflicts were forgotten, but the Cherokees in the West were now officially one people.

The Cherokee Nation continued to operate under the Constitution of 1839. The constitution provided for three branches of government—executive, legislative, and judicial. It affirmed the Cherokee practice of holding real estate in common while individuals owned improvements. The constitution also specified that improvements could be sold only to other Cherokees and that anyone moving out of the Nation forfeited his or her rights as a Cherokee.

Peace ushered in a period of remarkable achievement for the Cherokees. Many of the missionaries who had served the principal people in the East had gone west, where they helped the Cherokees reestablish churches and mission schools. Samuel A. Worcester, finally released from the Georgia penitentiary, continued to work on the translation of the New

Testament, hymnals, and other religious material into Cherokee. He had begun this work in the East in collaboration with Elias Boudinot and now he carried on alone.

In 1844, even before the signing of the peace treaty, the *Cherokee Advocate* began publication. Like its predecessor, the *Cherokee Phoenix*, the *Advocate* printed the laws of the Nation, national and international news, and advertisements in both English and Cherokee. Under the editorship of William P. Ross, nephew of the principal chief and a graduate of Princeton University, the *Advocate* carried a motto that expressed Cherokee nationalism and pride, "Our Rights—Our Country—Our Race."

During the 1840s, the Cherokees also established a system of public schools. The crowning achievement in education was the building of two seminaries (high schools), one for men and one for women, which opened their doors in 1851. The Female Seminary was particularly revolutionary. Most Anglo-Americans at the time believed that women were intellectually inferior to men, and so women had few opportunities to acquire any education beyond basic skills. The Cherokee Female Seminary was modeled after Mount Holyoke Female Seminary in Massachusetts (now Mount Holyoke College), perhaps the most radical educational institution at the time, which had been founded in 1837. The president of Mount Holyoke, Mary Lyon, assisted with the curriculum of the Cherokee Female Seminary, and graduates of the eastern women's college served as teachers at the seminary. (For additional information on this school, enter "Cherokee Female Seminary" into any search engine and browse the many sites listed.)

Unfortunately, worthy projects such as the seminaries were stymied by a lack of funds. Although the Constitution of 1839 contained a provision for taxation, the Cherokee government did not levy taxes. Instead, the government invested the money

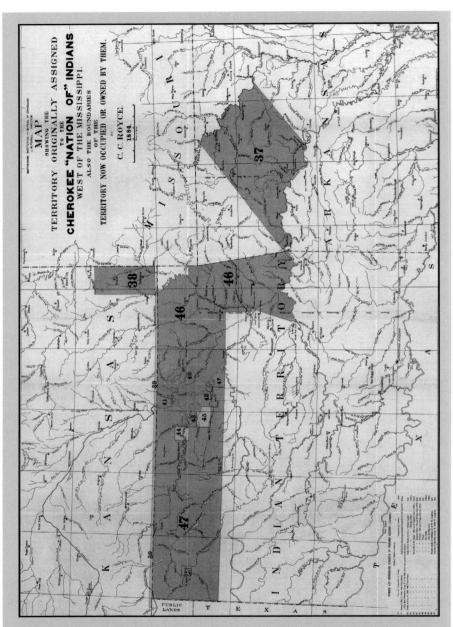

This 1884 map illustrates the lands occupied by the Cherokees to the west of the Mississippi River—some of the lands that became the Cherokee Nation after removal.

it had received as payment for land cessions, and the interest from this money supported the newspaper, schools, and other governmental operations. The problem was that expenditures, while not extravagant, exceeded income. The Cherokees tried to sell the Neutral Lands, an eight-hundred-thousand-acre tract on which no Cherokees lived, but the U.S. government offered them insultingly unfair terms. As the Nation's financial situation grew worse, the Cherokees reluctantly suspended publication of the *Advocate* and closed the seminaries. They would not resume operations until after the American Civil War (1861–1865).

The Cherokees built homes and farms in their new territory, and many of them prospered. By 1860, a total population of 21,000 Cherokees had 102,000 acres under cultivation. They owned 240,000 cattle, 20,000 horses and mules, and 15,000 hogs. As in the East, the standard of living among the Cherokees varied a great deal. Many of them erected simple one-room cabins and cultivated only a few acres but others constructed mansions and embarked on lucrative business ventures. Among the most profitable businesses were cattle ranching and salt production. Wealthy Cherokees had clear advantages in settling in Oklahoma: they had capital from the sale of their improvements in the East, and many brought with them their African slaves. In 1860, Cherokee planters owned four thousand slaves.

In the period when Cherokees were reestablishing themselves in the West, citizens of the United States were agonizing over the issue of slavery. In late 1860 and early 1861, the conflict over slavery came to a head when a coalition of Southern states seceded from the United States in order to form a separate nation, the Confederate States of America. This secession led directly to the American Civil War, which erupted in 1861.

The Civil War placed the Cherokees in an odd position because their laws legitimized the institution of slavery and their geographical location was in the South. Yet many Cherokees had serious misgivings about slavery, especially the traditionalists, who resented domination by a slaveholding elite. They regarded slavery not necessarily as a moral wrong but as a particularly unsavory feature of Anglo-American culture. In addition, Northern missionaries actively encouraged the abolition of slavery within the Cherokee Nation as well as the United States.

Many slaveholders respected these missionaries and were grateful for the schools and churches they had established, as well as the support they had given the Cherokees during the removal crisis. Furthermore, a number of slaveholders had little desire to ally themselves with the very Southerners who had demanded their removal. In 1861, Chief Ross expressed the Cherokees' dilemma to the council: "Our locality and situation ally us to the South, while to the North we are indebted for a defense of our rights in the past and that enlarged benevolence to which we owe our progress in civilization."

Traditionalists who favored abolition and even some slaveholders, such as Ross, preferred neutrality, a position they advocated in order to protect existing treaties between the U.S. government and the Cherokees. In the summer of 1861, Indian nations that neighbored the Cherokees signed treaties with the Confederacy. Because most Cherokee slaveholders favored a Confederate alliance, they encouraged Stand Watie to begin organizing a Cherokee company for the Confederate Army. Fearing a division of the Nation, John Ross signed a Confederate alliance in August 1861, and Cherokees officially enlisted in the Confederate Army.

One of the Cherokee soldiers' initial assignments was to aid in the capture of Opothle Yohola, a Creek chief. Although he was a wealthy slaveholder, Opothle Yohola opposed the

Creeks' Confederate alliance and decided to conduct a group of loyal Creeks, including women and children, to Kansas, which had not seceded, to take refuge behind Union lines. The Confederacy was determined to stop them. Cherokee traditionalists, in a regiment led by John Drew, refused to fight against fellow Indians whose views on the war they shared. The night before the battle was to take place, they fled their encampment. Some joined Opothle Yohola's flight, while others returned to their homes determined to fight for the Confederacy no more.

The Civil War in the United States so divided the Cherokees that they soon became embroiled in a parallel conflict of their own. The Unionist Cherokees, known as Pins, because their insignia was crossed pins worn under the lapel, attacked Confederate sympathizers and their property. The ardent Confederate Stand Watie and his supporters retaliated. Many Cherokees, including Hannah Hicks, the daughter of missionary Samuel A. Worcester, suffered from the repeated assaults of both Confederates and Pins. The Pins killed Hicks' Cherokee husband, a Unionist, by mistake, and Watie's men robbed her house. She wrote in her diary: "Alas, alas, for this miserable people, destroying each other as fast as they can." So many adult Cherokees died in this fighting that the construction of an orphanage became a priority after the war ended.

In the summer of 1862, U.S. forces invaded the Cherokee Nation. They took John Ross captive, but federal authorities soon paroled him. The principal chief then went east to spend the remainder of the war in Washington, D.C., and Philadelphia. Ross' support of the Confederacy had always been lukewarm at best, and he now became an advocate of Cherokee loyalty to the Union. Although Ross himself was too old to enlist in the military, three of his sons, three grandsons, and three nephews served in the U.S. Army during the Civil War.

When Ross left the Nation, Stand Watie saw an opportunity to redress old grievances. He promptly declared the office of principal chief vacant and assumed the position himself. Other Cherokee officials who had shifted their allegiance to the Union were removed from office and replaced by Watie supporters. This new government passed a conscription law and began drafting men into Confederate service. This meant that many men who had hoped to remain neutral during the Civil War were forced into hiding in order to avoid fighting for a cause they opposed in their hearts. While the men stayed in hiding, their families keenly felt the loss of their labor and suffered terrible poverty.

The majority of Cherokees refused to recognize the government headed by Watie and continued to regard Ross as principal chief. These dissenters met in council, revoked the Confederate treaty, and emancipated the slaves. Most slaveholders, however, had already moved their slaves south into the Choctaw Nation or northern Texas, so this act freed few slaves.

The Civil War ended in 1865, after Confederate General Robert E. Lee surrendered to Union General Ulysses S. Grant at Appomattox, Virginia, on April 9. But conflict continued within the Cherokee Nation until June 1865, when Brigadier General Stand Watie became the last Confederate general to surrender. This surrender did not, however, ensure a united Cherokee Nation.

When the Cherokee Union and Confederate representatives met with U.S. peace commissioners, the commissioners insisted that all Cherokees had been supporters of the Confederacy. Furthermore, they refused to recognize Ross as principal chief. In fact, Watie and the Confederate Cherokees received a far more cordial reception than Ross and the loyal Cherokees.

One reason for this new friendship was the willingness of the Confederate Cherokees to grant American railroad companies rights-of-way across the Cherokee Nation. In order to secure those rights-of-way, the United States seemed agreeable to a proposed division of the Cherokee Nation in which the railroads could lay tracks in the land "controlled" by Watie. How ironic it seemed to Ross that the United States had fought a war to preserve the Union only to permit a secession by southern Cherokees.

In the end, the Cherokees preserved their Nation and signed a treaty on August 11, 1865. The agreement extended citizenship rights to the freed slaves, permitted Delaware and Shawnee Indians to settle on Cherokee land, ceded the Neutral Lands to the United States, and granted rights-of-way to railroads.

The railroad rights-of-way spelled doom for the Cherokee Nation. Railroads competed to build their lines through the Cherokee Nation both to gain access to the cattle markets in Texas and to obtain sections of land along the construction routes. In the late nineteenth century, the U.S. government helped fund railroad construction by granting sections of public land to the railroads. Once the tracks had been laid, the line established, and the towns built along the route, land values along the railroad sky-rocketed. The railroads could then sell the land to help defray construction costs.

In the Cherokee Nation, however, public land did not belong to the United States but was held in common by the Cherokees. By promising the railroads free tracts of land, the U.S. government was giving away property it did not own. The railroads could take possession of this territory only when the Indian title was extinguished and the land reverted to the United States. Thus, the railroad owners, some of the wealthiest and most powerful men in the United States, came to view the Cherokee Nation as an obstacle to reaping additional profits and as an impediment to progress.

These wealthy industrialists were not alone in coveting Cherokee territory. The passage of the *Homestead Act* in 1862 gave many people in the United States hope of acquiring western land. This law awarded 160 acres for a nominal fee to anyone who settled and cultivated unoccupied lots for at least five years. Rapid population growth in the United States after the Civil War made whites eager to take advantage of the Homestead Act. They saw in Indian real estate, particularly in what is today Oklahoma, an opportunity for expansion and flooded into Oklahoma Territory, homesteading on ceded Indian tracts, such as the Cherokee Strip. These whites believed that they were justified in taking over Indian land because the Cherokees and other native peoples had far more acreage than they seemed to need or deserve.

Whites also poured into the Cherokee Nation as laborers on railroads and as workers in other enterprises, such as mining and logging. This created a chaotic situation because white people were not subject to the laws of the Cherokee Nation. Federal marshals tried to keep the peace, but they were overworked and resented. The turmoil made the Cherokee Nation a haven for outlaws and led many people to support the extension of U.S. law over Indian Territory, which would bring an end to Indian self-government.

A new generation of philanthropists, influenced by those who had once prescribed the civilization program as the antidote to Indian troubles, expressed their distress that Native peoples seemed to be as attached to their own nations and ways of life as ever. In the name of "saving the Cherokee," they began to advocate assimilation once again. The best method to accomplish this goal seemed to be the termination of tribal ownership of land and the *allotment* of 160-acre tracts to individuals. "Surplus" land would be opened to white settlement.

These "friends of the Indian" believed that if Native people had privately owned farms, they would soon abandon their Indian ways and become acculturated into white society. Because most Native peoples held their land in common and their governments rested on that principle, a division of Indian land would bring about an end to Indian nations. Railroad companies, of course, supported the dissolution of Indian governments because that was the only way that they could exploit their land grants. White homesteaders anticipated carving farms out of the remaining territory.

Unable to resist economic and "philanthropic" pressure, the U.S. Congress passed the *General Allotment Act* in 1887, often called the *Dawes Act* after its sponsor, Henry L. Dawes. This legislation divided up Indian land once held in common by Native peoples, allotted it to them as individuals, opened surplus land to white settlement, and brought Indian peoples under federal jurisdiction. In order to offer some protection to traditionalists, who were unaccustomed to private land ownership, the act restricted sale of individual allotments for twenty-five years.

The Dawes Act exempted the Cherokees and a few other groups from allotment, but in 1893, Congress directed President Grover Cleveland to appoint commissioners to negotiate allotment agreements with those peoples. During the next three years, Congress authorized the survey of Indian land and the compilation of official rolls, lists of those Indians entitled to receive allotments. The Cherokees steadfastly refused to negotiate, but they could do little else to resist allotment.

The Cherokees were handicapped in their resistance because their national treasury was empty. After the Civil War, the Cherokees had supported the Nation by leasing the Cherokee Strip (or Outlet) to white ranchers. In 1890, the U.S. government closed the Strip to cattlemen, and the Cherokee government lost its major source of income. In 1893, the

Cherokees were compelled to sell the land to the United States for $1.40 per acre, and the Strip was opened to white settlement under the provisions of the Homestead Act.

The Cherokees continued to oppose allotment and declined to cooperate with the Dawes Commission when it arrived to prepare the official Cherokee roll. Congress authorized the commission to continue without tribal cooperation. When Cherokees refused to appear before the commission to select their allotments, the commission assigned plots of land to them. Finally, in the Curtis Act of 1898, Congress ended Indian land tenure without the Indians' consent in preparation for the admission of the state of Oklahoma to the Union in 1907. Having no real alternative, the practically defunct Cherokee Nation agreed to allotment in 1902, virtually after the fact. Although the Cherokee Nation presumably had ceased to exist, the tribe continued to have assets, such as the proceeds from the sale of town lots. The necessity of having someone represent the Cherokee people, who were entitled to these assets, forced the United States to appoint chiefs, but these officials had little power until the 1970s.

The Cherokees and other Native peoples who originally lived in the South (often called "the five civilized tribes") opposed the creation of the state of Oklahoma. In 1905, representatives of these Indian nations drafted a constitution for a proposed Indian state to be called Sequoyah. The state of Sequoyah included the land in the eastern half of what was to become Oklahoma that belonged to the Chickasaws, Choctaws, Creeks, and Seminoles as well as the Cherokees. Congress tabled the constitution, thereby rejecting the admission of Sequoyah to the Union, and held to its timetable that allotment must be completed and tribal governments dissolved by 1906.

In 1907, the state of Oklahoma was admitted to the Union. As part of the celebration, a mock wedding took place between an Indian woman and a cowboy, symbolizing the marriage of two cultures. This ceremony was not an accurate representation of Oklahoma statehood. Indians, who had once held title to the entire state, were now a minority. Their own laws abolished, Indians found themselves dominated and exploited. Contrary to the hopes of capitalists and philanthropists, however, the Cherokees and other Native peoples in Oklahoma did not disappear—nor did their traditions, values, and even nations.

6

The Eastern Band of Cherokees

N ot all Cherokees living in the East traveled the Trail of Tears west of the Mississippi in the early nineteenth century. After removal, a community of Cherokees numbering approximately one thousand remained behind in the remote mountains of western North Carolina. These people came to be known as the Eastern Band of Cherokee Indians. They traced their origins to the Treaty of 1819, which permitted Cherokees living within ceded territory to register for individual reservations of 640 acres and become American citizens.

Forty-nine families in North Carolina chose to remain on their land rather than move across the Little Tennessee River, which had become the boundary of the Cherokee Nation. These Cherokees felt little regret over severing their formal ties to the Cherokee Nation and becoming citizens of the state of North Carolina. In many ways, they had resisted changes in their traditional way of life. The "civilization" program of the U.S. government and the Christianization efforts of missionaries had had relatively little impact on them. They preferred traditional government, education, and religion over the republican government, Christianity, and mission schools advocated by the leaders of the Cherokee Nation. Most of all, they wanted to continue to hunt in the forests where Kana'ti had found game, to farm the fields darkened by Selu's blood, and to fish in the rivers that had given birth to Wild Boy.

Unfortunately, these Cherokees experienced the same difficulties as others who received reservations under the terms of the Treaty of 1819. North Carolina had already disposed of the reservations granted to the eastern Cherokees by the federal government. North Carolina, however, admitted the error and paid the Cherokees for their land. A few Cherokees, including Euchella, a prominent local leader, took the money and moved their families across the Little Tennessee into the Cherokee Nation. Others, however, chose to stay in North Carolina. Under the leadership of Yonaguska, they bought land along the Oconaluftee River and supported themselves by selling livestock and ginseng, a medicinal herb, to white traders.

The Oconaluftee Cherokees, as they were known in the early nineteenth century, had little experience dealing with the non-Cherokee world. Few spoke English or had other skills necessary for protecting their land and themselves from whites who greedily eyed their territory. Fortunately, they found a spokesman in William Holland Thomas, a fatherless white boy whom Yonaguska had adopted. When he grew up, Thomas became a trader, and he helped the Cherokees consolidate their landholdings by purchasing tracts for them as the land became available. When the removal treaty was signed in 1835, the Oconaluftee Cherokees insisted that it did not apply to them because they were no longer part of the Cherokee Nation. Instead, they were citizens of North Carolina. Thomas went to Washington, D.C., to lobby on their behalf and pleaded their case before the North Carolina legislature.

In the end, his efforts helped save the Oconaluftee Cherokees from removal. North Carolina tacitly assented to their remaining in the state, and the United States also informally recognized their rights under earlier treaties. Nevertheless, the position of the Oconaluftee Cherokees was precarious. Although they had considerable sympathy for those Cherokees who were being hunted by soldiers, imprisoned in stockades, and marched off to the West, any aid to the victims jeopardized their own status.

Tension increased when citizens of the Cherokee Nation, a man named Tsali and his sons, killed two soldiers involved in the Cherokee roundup and wounded another. They then fled with their wives and children into the mountains. General Winfield Scott insisted that these Cherokees must be punished. In order to secure their own position, the Oconaluftee Cherokees agreed to assist in the capture of Tsali's band.

Thomas and the Oconaluftees enlisted the aid of Euchella, Yonaguska's son-in-law, who was subject to removal because he had moved back into the Cherokee Nation. These Cherokees captured Tsali's band and executed the murderers. Oral tradition suggests that they did this reluctantly and that Tsali recognized the necessity of their actions and faced his executioners courageously. Because of his assistance in capturing Tsali's band, Euchella received permission to remain with the Oconaluftee Cherokees. General Scott also withdrew the soldiers and, thus, other fugitives were able to come out of hiding. More than a thousand Cherokees managed to remain in North Carolina.

The descendants of fugitives, Euchella, and the Oconaluftees became the Eastern Band of Cherokees. They forged a common identity, in part by retelling the story of Tsali, a Cherokee who loved his country so much that he was willing to kill rather than leave and to die so that other Cherokees could remain in their homeland. Although many versions of the account do not bear up under close historical scrutiny, Tsali has become a folk hero who embodies the deep attachment eastern Cherokees feel for their land.

The desire to remain in the East is a recurring theme throughout the history of the Eastern Band. Nevertheless, the federal government made periodic attempts to convince them to join their relatives in the West. These attempts usually stemmed from the government's wish to clarify the status of the Cherokees or to simplify the administration of Indian policy. Occasionally, groups of Cherokees went west looking for better opportunities or to escape political factionalism at home. Most eastern Cherokees, however, were determined to stay exactly where they were.

After removal, the lives of eastern Cherokees changed little until the Civil War. William H. Thomas was an enthusiastic supporter of the Confederacy, and he convinced more than two hundred Cherokees to enlist in a legion he was organizing for the Confederate Army. Joining Thomas out of personal commitment rather than political sentiment, the Cherokees primarily served to defend eastern Tennessee and western North Carolina.

In 1864, a Union force captured between twenty and thirty members of Thomas' legion. In a prison camp in Knoxville, Tennessee, many of these Cherokees learned for the first time that they had been defending the right of the South to uphold slavery. Some prisoners, owning no slaves and having little sympathy for wealthy planters, renounced their allegiance to the Confederacy. When they received federal pardons, they joined the Union Army. A few Cherokees, therefore, actually became veterans of both the Confederate and Union armies. When the Union veterans returned home after the war, they encountered considerable hostility from those who had remained loyal to Thomas and his legion.

The period of Reconstruction immediately following the Civil War brought major changes to the Cherokee people. Under the newly devised Reconstruction Constitution of North Carolina, they acquired the right to vote, and some began to exercise that right in the counties where they lived. In 1868, the

Cherokees also wrote their own constitution and, despite considerable factionalism, elected a chief and council. In the same year, the federal government recognized the eastern Cherokees as an Indian tribe distinct from the western Cherokees.

At this point, the Cherokees certainly needed the protection that a formal political system and federal recognition would help ensure. William Holland Thomas' business ventures had suffered as a result of the war and his health failed. Thomas' creditors began to seize his property. Unfortunately, Thomas held title to land he had bought for the Cherokees, but his illness prevented him from sorting out who actually owned what. His creditors, of course, assumed that any property in Thomas' name belonged to him and seized it in payment of his debts. Some of the land, however, had already been paid for by the Cherokees, although the deed had not yet been assigned to them.

The United States instituted a lawsuit on behalf of the Cherokees. The court awarded much of the land in question to the Cherokees, and the federal government accepted the title in trust. This meant that the Cherokees owned the land but could not sell it without federal approval. Although more acculturated Cherokees sometimes resented federal control of their land, the trusteeship offered the eastern Cherokees some protection from land-hungry whites who were beginning to show interest in the Indians' rugged mountain homeland.

The Cherokees' new relationship with the federal government brought a number of social changes, particularly in education. Before the Civil War, parents had taught their children the Sequoyah syllabary at home but few children received a formal education in the English language. After the war, the United States arranged for a few students to attend boarding school but many became homesick, particularly when racial prejudice led whites in the schools to treat them as inferiors.

In 1881, Quakers from Indiana contracted with the Eastern Band to provide a school system. They established day schools in several communities and a boarding school in what is today the town of Cherokee, North Carolina. This arrangement sparked a controversy that centered around the Quakers' political leanings. In 1892, the federal government took over the educational system.

Both Quakers and federal teachers attempted to eradicate traditional Cherokee practices and beliefs among their students. They forced Cherokees to speak English and washed children's mouths out with soap if they used their Native language. Only decades later did the educational system come to value the Cherokees' own heritage.

The attempt to destroy Cherokee culture and assimilate Native people was no more successful in North Carolina than it was in Oklahoma. Many Cherokees found their way of life preferable to that of white Americans and sought to preserve it, accepting change when they could carefully direct it. For example, the Cherokees no longer had independent villages with councils. Instead, they established the gadugi, or work company, defined by anthropologist John Witthoft as "the social survival of the Cherokee town, carrying on the economic functions of the town long after its political functions were lost."

Members of the gadugi worked together on each person's land, and if someone was sick, the gadugi did his or her work for him. The gadugi also worked for nonmembers and used the proceeds from their labors to fund various projects or to pay for members' funerals. The gadugi embodied the communal values of traditional Cherokee culture and applied them to the modern world.

Swimmer, a Cherokee medicine man of considerable ability, also represented continuity between the past and the future. For more than a decade before his death in 1899, Swimmer shared his knowledge with anthropologist James Mooney. Mooney recorded Swimmer's stories about how the earth was made and about Kana'ti and Selu. Swimmer also

Swimmer was a skilled Cherokee medicine man. Thanks to his many conversations with anthropologist James Mooney, his knowledge of Cherokee history and healing traditions were preserved for future generations.

revealed to Mooney his sacred formulas. These were prescriptions for curing illness, charms for hunting, and love potions that he had recorded carefully in the Sequoyah syllabary. Swimmer permitted Mooney to present these records to the Smithsonian Institution in Washington, D.C., because he feared that they otherwise might be lost to a younger generation who no longer valued traditional ways. (For additional information on Mooney, enter "Anthropologist James Mooney" into any search engine and browse the many sites listed.)

Although traditional culture remained strong, Cherokee leaders in the post–Civil War period were more adept at dealing with the non-Cherokee world than their predecessors. They began to look for ways to expand the tribal domain and services. One possible source of funds was money derived from the sale of the Neutral Lands in the West. The eastern Cherokees sued their western brothers for a share in the proceeds of the sale. In 1886, the U.S. Supreme Court ruled that the eastern Cherokees had severed their formal ties to the Cherokee Nation in their refusal to emigrate west and had no right to share in the Nation's income. The Court went on to state that the eastern Cherokees did not, in fact, compose a tribe but were instead merely citizens of the state of North Carolina. This ruling caused the Cherokees considerable consternation. They were disappointed that no money would be forthcoming, but more alarming was the Court's ruling that they were not a tribe.

Confusion stemming from the Court ruling engulfed the eastern Cherokees just as politically powerful whites in North Carolina began to raise objections to the Indians' maintaining rights of citizenship. The state's dominant party, the Democrats, had always counted on the Cherokees' allegiance at election time. Their loyalty went unquestioned until 1884, when the Eastern Band unexpectedly shifted to the Republican side and cast their votes for James G. Blaine, the Republican nominee in that year's presidential election.

North Carolina Democrats saw the Cherokees' support of a Republican candidate as a slap in the face. The Cherokees' hold on the balance of power between the two parties in local counties exacerbated the situation. North Carolina Democrats looked for ways to disfranchise the Cherokees, thus jeopardizing their legal status. Were they really citizens of the state? Were they entitled to enjoy the privileges of citizenship, such as voting? Or were they merely wards of the federal government, which held their lands in trust and administered their affairs? The Supreme Court had suggested that the Cherokees in the East did not constitute a tribe, yet Congress had recognized them as a distinct tribe in 1868, and the federal government had treated the Eastern Band as though it were a tribe.

The eastern Cherokee chief in the 1880s, Nimrod Jarrett Smith, countered these threats with an ingenious move that solidified the legal status of the Cherokees and provided some protection under state law. He applied to the North Carolina legislature for a corporate charter, which was awarded in 1889. This charter made the Eastern Band of Cherokee Indians a corporation. As such, they could enter into contracts, own property, manage their assets, and bring suit in court. The corporate charter gave the Cherokees considerable protection in an age when the rights of corporations were regarded as almost inviolable. The charter provided for the administration of the corporation, and it is under this charter (with revisions and modifications) that the eastern Cherokees have governed themselves ever since.

The corporate charter did not, however, end the Cherokees' problems. The tribal council faced serious difficulties with property taxes owed to the counties in which it held land. One way of paying outstanding taxes and redeeming land already seized for nonpayment was selling timber on tribal land. The council, acting as a corporation, entered into a contract for sale of the timber. The federal government, treating Cherokees as wards, made other arrangements for the sale of the timber. Ultimately, the case ended up in court. In 1895, a federal court ruled that the Indians were indeed wards, not citizens, and that they could not sell their timber independently.

Although the timber transaction ultimately was resolved satisfactorily, the case had far-reaching effects for the Cherokees. Democrats, who held the majority in North Carolina, remembered the Republican votes cast by the Cherokees. Democratic politicians decided that if the Cherokees were wards and not citizens, then they could no longer vote. In 1900, the state refused to permit Cherokees to vote; they did not regain that right until 1930 and did not exercise it freely until after World War II.

The timber sale took place at the very same time that the U.S. Congress provided for the allotment of Indian land to individuals, in effect ending Indian governments. The federal government was in the process of forcing allotment on the western Cherokees. Many people in North Carolina expected the same policy to be applied to the Eastern Band with tracts of land *and* proceeds from the timber sale going to individuals. In anticipation of the division of Cherokee funds among members of the band, many whites deceitfully managed to get their names on the official roll. They were disappointed: Allotment did not come to the Eastern Band. Nevertheless, these "white Cherokees" benefited from their enrollment, frequently at the expense of true Cherokees. Federal trustee-ship prevented non-Cherokees from buying Cherokee land, but this provision did not apply to "white Cherokees," who soon came to dominate the economic life of the Eastern Band, becoming prominent figures in Cherokee politics as well.

The Eastern Band entered the twentieth century as a far more diverse group than it had been when its members escaped removal to the West. No longer isolated from the dominant American culture, they struggled to protect their land and their society from the world at large, and from the internal dishar-mony that plagued them. As the Eastern Band moved into the twentieth century, they asked themselves if they could survive in the modern world.

7

Cherokees in Modern America

B y the early twentieth century, the Cherokees had become extremely diverse. They had distinct tribal governments in Oklahoma and North Carolina, separated by half a continent. Some Cherokees had embraced the message of missionaries and philanthropists: they spoke English as their only language, attended Christian churches, and participated aggressively in a world economic system. Other Cherokees preferred their own language, values, and religion to those of Anglo-America. Most Cherokees, however, fell somewhere in between. Never abandoning their identity as Cherokee, they adapted to political and economic change in a dizzying variety of ways, and the tribes developed legal definitions of "Cherokee" that enabled them to accommodate their increasingly varied citizenry. Despite Cherokee diversity, a respect and appreciation for traditional ways has been rekindled in recent decades, and the

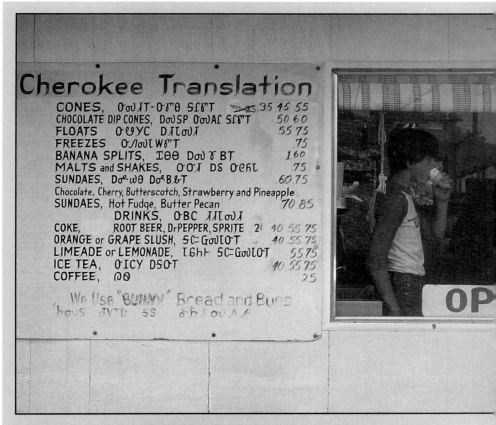

Today, the Cherokees' determination to hold onto their native culture can be seen in many forms. For example, this restaurant's menu is presented in both English and Cherokee, a sign that both languages are considered equally necessary in Cherokee lands.

survival of Cherokee culture has become a source of strength and pride for all of the principal people.

In the West, the United States forced allotment on the Cherokees in the 1890s. The Cherokee Nation opposed allotment until it really had no choice but to concede. Most Cherokees reluctantly accepted the policy, settled on their allotments, and participated in the governance of the new state of Oklahoma. The Cherokee Robert Latham Owen was one of the first two Oklahomans elected to the U.S. Senate in

1907, and Cherokees have continued to participate in politics at the state and national levels.

Some western Cherokees, however, felt estranged from the new state and turned to the Keetoowah Society, a traditionalist organization that gave rise to the Pins of the Civil War era. Under the leadership of Red Bird Smith, they retreated to the hills of eastern Oklahoma and took spiritual refuge in traditional teachings and practices. Initially, they refused to accept allotments, live on tracts assigned to them, or have anything to do with the new political and economic order. The United States had Smith arrested for refusal to accept allotment and forced him to comply under protest. In 1905, Smith renounced participation of the Keetoowah Society in politics, although individual members could participate as they chose. At this point, the Keetoowah Society, which later became known as the Nighthawk Keetoowahs, wrote a constitution proclaiming its religious focus. Those who chose to remain politically active incorporated as the Keetoowah Society, Inc. In the twenty-first century, Nighthawk Keetoowahs maintain stomp grounds where they conduct ceremonies, while the United Keetoowah Band, federally recognized as a tribe in 1946, traces its descent from the Keetoowah Society, Inc.

Other Oklahoma residents generally showed interest in Cherokees only when an opportunity to exploit them surfaced. For example, many Cherokees became the victims of unscrupulous individuals who appointed themselves guardians for the estates of Indians who could not or would not manage their allotments. Unlike neighboring Creeks and Osages, the Cherokees had little oil on their lands, but the marketability of timber, minerals, and other resources led to gross abuses of the office of guardian. Many Indians were defrauded of their estates by people who were supposed to be their protectors. Kate Barnard, commissioner of Oklahoma's Office of Charities and Corrections, was one of

Cherokee artists today continue to carve the traditional masks used for ceremony by their ancestors. Sometimes, carvers use skins or gourds to create masks, but most are carved from wood and colored with paint, clay, charcoal, or other types of dyes. This particular mask, a common type among the Cherokees, is called a buffalo mask. It depicts the fact of a man with horns.

Masks like this one were worn during the Cherokees' Booger Dance, which was performed as a way to express their views regarding the perceived peculiarities of other Indian cultures and Europeans.

Soapstone pipes, which often depict animals or other natural objects, are among the most commonly found ancient Cherokee artifacts. The Cherokees are renowned for their beautiful and unique carvings, and there is a great demand for pipes like this one among collectors of ancient cultural objects.

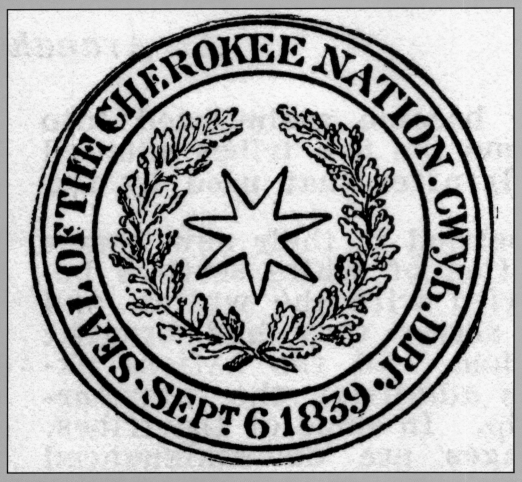

The official seal of the Cherokee Nation (seen here) was adopted in 1871. Its design echoes the early government systems and the ongoing survival of the Cherokee people. The seven-pointed star has several meanings. It represents the seven ancient clans of the Cherokees and the seven characters of Sequoyah's syllabary that stand for "Cherokee Nation." The wreath of oak leaves symbolizes the sacred fire that the Cherokees have always kept burning. The wording in the margins declares the authority of the seal in both the English and the Cherokee languages.

This Cherokee woman is weaving a basket in the method that has been used by the tribe for centuries. Through the efforts of older Cherokees who are skilled in the ancient arts and customs, younger generations are learning about their heritage and are finding ways to preserve Cherokee traditions even in the modern world.

Mask carvers are among the best known of the Cherokee artists. As they live and work on the reservation, they are refining the techniques that have been used by ceremonial artisans since before history was recorded.

Though Cherokee masks are sometimes carved out of skins or gourds, the majority are carved from wood such as buckeye and then colored with natural dyes, paint, clay, charcoal, or shoe polish.

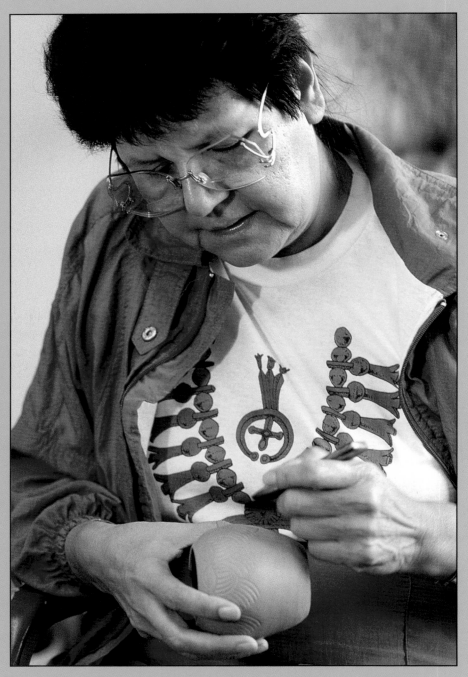

Elizabeth Bigmeat Maney continues the tradition of Cherokee potters. Maney's sister, Louise, has several pieces that appear in the Smithsonian Institution's collection.

the few public officials to recognize and speak out against the abuses of guardians:

> I have been compelled to see orphans robbed, starved, and buried for money. I have named the men and accused them and furnished the records and affidavits to convict them, but with no result. I decided long ago that Oklahoma had no citizen who cared whether or not an orphan is robbed or starved or killed—because his dead claim is easier to handle than if he were alive.

The swindles of guardians contributed dramatically to the loss of Indian land. In 1891, western Cherokees had owned 19,500,000 acres; by 1971, Cherokees held only 146,598 acres in Oklahoma.

The much smaller Eastern Band of Cherokees managed to keep a land base of more than 56,000 acres in western North Carolina. Most Cherokees lived on Qualla Boundary, a 44,000-acre tract in Jackson and Swain counties but others lived nearby on scattered parcels in Swain, Cherokee, and Graham counties. Despite their extensive holdings, the political and economic position of the Eastern Band remained precarious. Disfranchised by the state in 1900, the eastern Cherokees hoped that their right to vote would automatically be restored when, in 1924, the federal government extended citizenship rights to all Native Americans who had not previously enjoyed them. But North Carolina officials insisted that members of the Eastern Band could not be made citizens until their land had been allotted. Finally, in 1930, Congress passed "an Act to confer full rights of citizenship upon the Cherokee Indians resident in the State of North Carolina." Yet even this precise language did not convince local county election boards that the Cherokees enjoyed the right of suffrage, and few Cherokees were allowed to register to vote before World War II.

In the early twentieth century, the timber industry and related enterprises dominated the economy of western North

Carolina. The Cherokees had sold their best timber at the end of the nineteenth century, but the sale of pulp wood and tanbark continued into the 1920s, and provided employment for some Cherokees. Although they benefited from steady employment, the Cherokees suffered prejudice and discrimination. According to anthropologist John Witthoft, Cherokee workers received only 35 cents a day, while whites were paid $1 a day.

When the timber boom ended in the mid-1920s, the North Carolina Cherokees found themselves without any prospect of future employment. Furthermore, the dramatic increase in the Cherokee population at the turn of the twentieth century— produced by the enrollment of avaricious whites onto official rolls—strained resources. "White Cherokees" had come to control the Eastern Band's most fertile land, pushing traditionalists into remote coves or onto treeless, eroded hillsides. Reduced to subsistence farming, many barely survived. By the mid-1930s the New Deal, an economic reform program introduced by President Franklin D. Roosevelt, had brought some relief to the Eastern Band. Cherokees participated in various work-relief programs, including the Works Progress Administration and the National Youth Administration. In addition, approximately one hundred Cherokee men received two weeks of work per month from the Indian Emergency Conservation Work Program. This program focused on conserving natural resources, and projects in western North Carolina included the improvement of roads and the construction of horse and truck trails.

The opening of the Great Smoky Mountains National Park in 1934 was a momentous event for the Eastern Band. The federal government believed that the Indians of Qualla Boundary, which adjoined the park, could serve as a tourist attraction and originally intended to integrate them into the park. When the Cherokees successfully resisted this plan, the government helped Native artisans organize a cooperative to market their baskets, pottery, woodcarvings, and other crafts.

The park brought thousands of tourists to the region and gave the Eastern Band a new source of income through the sale of souvenirs. The influx of whites also permanently changed the lives of the eastern Cherokees by thrusting them into daily contact with Americans from across the country. By the late 1980s, more people visited the Great Smoky Mountains than any other national park, with most entering or leaving the park through Qualla Boundary.

The Roosevelt administration's impact on the Cherokees was not limited to New Deal programs and the opening of the park. In 1933, the president appointed John Collier, a sociologist with a long history of defending Indian rights, to the post of Commissioner of Indian Affairs. Collier secured passage of the *Indian Reorganization Act* (IRA), also known as the Wheeler–Howard Act, which officially recognized that the allotment program had been a disaster for Native peoples. This legislation ended the process of allotment, banned the unregulated sale of Indian lands, and authorized the appropriation of $2 million a year to purchase land for Indians. The act also permitted the organization of Indian governments and sanctioned the incorporation of Native peoples. These provisions made it possible for Indians to direct their own economic development and to appear as a legal entity in court. Collier viewed the bill as "the beginning in the process of liberating and rejuvenating a subjugated and exploited race in the midst of an aggressive civilization."

Although the Indian Reorganization Act set a new sympathetic tone for Indian relations with the federal government, the legislation had little actual effect on the principal people in the East or in the West. In the East, the act's condemnation of allotment angered many "white Cherokees" who had hoped to profit from the dissolution of the Eastern Band's land base. They continued to promote individual ownership of land. This produced deep factionalism among the eastern Cherokees because traditionalists tended to favor their communal land system, which Collier sought to protect.

Because of political pressure in Oklahoma, the Indian Reorganization Act overlooked the western Cherokees and other Native peoples in that state. In 1936, however, Congress passed the Oklahoma Indian Welfare Act, which gave Oklahoma Indians the right to adopt constitutions and secure corporate charters. This legislation provided for the federal purchase of land to be held in trust for incorporated Oklahoma Indians. The government also made loans to various Indian economic development projects, including one promising plan to grow and market strawberries. Yet by 1936, many Cherokees had left eastern Oklahoma, fleeing the dust bowl for new lives in California and elsewhere. An Indian nation with a communally owned land where its citizens resided might have been legally possible, but it seemed unlikely. The only Cherokees living on a reservation—communally held *trust lands*—remained those in North Carolina, whose lands had not been allotted to individuals.

In 1946, Congress authorized the organization of the United Keetoowah Band of Cherokees under the provisions of the Oklahoma Indian Welfare Act. By 1950, the tribe had compiled a roll of members and had written a constitution that the *Bureau of Indian Affairs* accepted. Although most members of the UKB are also eligible for citizenship in the Cherokee Nation, which traces its membership solely from the Dawes Rolls that were prepared for allotments, the UKB is a separate tribe with its own tribal government and enterprises. In 1990, the UKB enacted legislation that prohibited dual tribal membership for all new enrollees, but it permitted those who already held dual memberships to continue to do so. The Cherokee Nation has imposed no such restriction.

New Deal programs brought less prosperity to western Cherokees than to their relatives in the East. No equivalent of the Great Smoky Mountains National Park promised a long-term solution to their economic problems. Nevertheless, agricultural agents funded by the federal government introduced scientific farming techniques, while their female counterparts, home-demonstration agents, instructed women in food preparation, hygiene, and child care. New school programs provided educational opportunities for Indian children. Poverty in many Cherokee communities, however, was so profound that these measures had limited impact.

World War II did bring significant changes to the Cherokees. As in World War I, many Cherokees enlisted in the armed forces. Like World War I, this conflict took a generation of young Cherokees beyond the circumscribed world of their Indian communities and introduced them not only to a broader American society but also to that of Europe. In World War II, more than a thousand Cherokees fought alongside fellow Americans of all races and ethnicities. Some had been drafted by the armed forces, but the majority had volunteered. After the war, the G.I. Bill helped many Cherokee veterans to attend college free of charge. Furthermore, in 1946, Cherokee veterans in North Carolina finally forced county registrars to permit them to vote.

By the 1950s, many Cherokees had broadened their horizons and moved from their communities or reservation into urban centers throughout the United States. This shift from the country to the city resulted from a federal relocation program instituted by the Bureau of Indian Affairs. The bureau instituted job training programs in industrialized cities, sometimes offering to teach Indians directly, sometimes paying their tuition at a vocational school. The "new" policy of drawing Indians from reservations reflected a philosophy operative since the nineteenth century that assumed Native Americans would fare best by moving into mainstream society.

As in the past, the federal program of the 1950s met with both praise and criticism. Advocates of relocation argued that by leaving their enclaves Indians would gain the same economic opportunities that other Americans enjoyed. The policy's detractors accused the government of acting out of self-interest. They asserted that the United States cared little about Indian welfare and wanted to move Native Americans into cities in order to reduce the cost of administering federally sponsored programs on the reservations. Indeed, many tribes suffered terribly upon entering cities because they lost many of the benefits, such as free health care and education, which the government had once provided. The Oklahoma Cherokees, in particular, fell on hard times. Many moved out of their rural communities and into urban slums where they worked at menial jobs and suffered racial discrimination from whites.

The overall economic conditions for the Cherokees living in North Carolina and Oklahoma slowly began to improve in the 1950s and 1960s, largely through community action programs. The Eastern Band established the Cherokee Tribal Community Services program in 1952 and imposed a sales tax to finance fire and police protection, garbage collection, and sewer and water lines. The western Cherokees found funds to finance their own development in 1961 when the Indian Claims Commission, which had been established in 1946 to settle claims against the U.S. government, awarded them $15 million for the forced sale of the Cherokee Strip in 1893 to the federal government. Although the money was paid on a per-capita basis to descendants of Cherokees on the official roll, the Cherokee Nation retained the interest that accrued during the five to seven years it took to locate and pay individual recipients. Furthermore, payments of those who had no heirs or could not be located went to the Cherokee Nation. These funds permitted tribal government to operate for the first time since Oklahoma became a state. In addition, Chief W.W. Keeler established a private foundation that helped finance the construction of a cultural center and land purchases.

Self-help projects found additional stimulus in the Great Society programs devised by the Johnson administration in the 1960s to end poverty in the United States. The Eastern Band, for example, obtained funding to build and refurbish housing. According to anthropologist John Witthoft, in 1946, ninety percent of the houses on Qualla Boundary were hardly fit for people to live in. By the 1970s, substandard housing had been reduced to fifty percent—not an enviable percentage but certainly an improvement. Among the western Cherokees also, federal funds provided better housing and sanitation.

These programs, however, did not entirely solve the problems facing the Cherokees. During the 1960s, deep cultural divisions remained, especially between traditional Oklahoma Cherokees and the assimilated western Cherokees, who held the greatest sway over tribal affairs. Traditional Cherokees, who numbered approximately 11,000 during this period, organized to assert their rights, creating an informal organization, the Five County Northeastern Oklahoma Cherokee Organization, to voice their concerns about economic and cultural exploitation. The movement lasted only from 1965 to 1973, but it succeeded in calling attention to the plight of traditional Cherokees and demanding that Cherokee leaders include them in their development plans.

Other political changes have occurred within the Cherokee Nation. In 1971, citizens of the Cherokee Nation voted for principal chief for the first time since Oklahoma became a state, and in 1976, they enacted a new constitution that provided for the election of tribal officials, permanently ending the practice of presidential appointment. The democratization of the Cherokee Nation gave Oklahoma Cherokees the formal voice in tribal affairs they had been denied. Exercising limited jurisdiction over fourteen counties in northeastern Oklahoma, the revitalized Cherokee Nation developed a complex of businesses, programs, and services. By 2003, the Cherokee Nation had more than 220,000 members, tribal assets of more than $135.6 million (excluding Cherokee Nation Enterprises and Cherokee Nation Industries), and an operating budget of more than $264 million.

New opportunities and a renewed commitment to traditional communities drew many Cherokees back to Oklahoma. One of these was Wilma Mankiller, whose family had relocated to San Francisco when she was a child. In 1975, she came home to Oklahoma. Mankiller became active in community development projects, particularly one that brought water to remote Cherokee communities. The Cherokees elected her vice chief and then principal chief of the Cherokee Nation. Chief Mankiller, who grew up far away from her Cherokee homeland, embodies a new concern for Cherokee culture and for those people actively preserving it. (For additional information on the Cherokees' first female principal chief, enter "Wilma Mankiller" into any search engine and browse the many sites listed.)

Unlike their western brethren, citizens of the Eastern Band encountered obstacles in their attempts to improve life on their reservation. Because the eastern Cherokees did not have clear title to their land (the federal government holds it in trust), businesses were reluctant to invest money within Qualla Boundary. This situation retarded economic development and forced many Cherokees to depend on the seasonal tourist industry for their income.

In order to be successful, these Cherokees had to provide tourists with a stereotypical view of Indians, featuring a lifestyle that included tipis and warbonnets, items Cherokees never traditionally used. In recent years, however, a museum, a living history village, and several other attractions have presented a more authentic account of Cherokee history and culture. Unfortunately, tourism did not solve all the economic problems of the eastern Cherokees. Unemployment continued to soar each winter, and in the 1970s, the average income of the eight thousand North Carolina Cherokees was only sixty percent of the national average.

Wilma Mankiller, who was born in 1945 in Tahlequah, Oklahoma, was elected the first female principal chief of the Cherokee Nation in 1985. Her election reflected the traditionally high status that women hold in Cherokee society.

In the 1980s, the eastern Cherokees began to explore innovative and controversial solutions to their economic problems. Since its title is held in trust by the federal government, Qualla Boundary is not subject to state regulatory laws prohibiting gambling. Taking advantage of this status, a group of Cherokee businessmen built a high-stakes bingo parlor to attract players from throughout the nation. On opening night in 1982, Cherokee bingo attracted four thousand players from as far away as Philadelphia, Miami, and even Canada. The reduction of federal support for many reservation programs in the 1980s fueled interest in Indian gaming throughout the country. When the United States Supreme Court ruled in 1987 that, as long as the state permitted some kind of gambling, Indian casinos were legal, Congress passed the *Indian Gaming Regulatory Act* the following year. This law required a reservation to negotiate a compact with the state in order to have Class III gaming, which includes casino-style dice and card games as well as most machine gaming.

After years of legal wrangling with the reluctant North Carolina governor, the Eastern Band signed a gaming compact with the state. In 1995, the Eastern Band entered into a

Wilma Mankiller Speaks Out about How to Improve Cherokees' Lives, April 2, 1993

I think first it's important before I start talking about what we're doing today in the 1990's and what we did throughout the eighties or even the seventies in rebuilding our tribe; I think it's really, really important to put our current work and our current issues in a historical context. I can't tell you how many everyday Americans that I've talked with who've visited a tribal community in Oklahoma or in other places, and they've looked around and they saw all the social indicators of decline: high infant mortality, high unemployment, many, many other very serious problems among our people, and they always ask, "What happened to these people? Why do Native people have all these problems?", and I think that in order to understand the contemporary issues we're dealing with today and how we plan to dig our way out and how indeed we are digging our way out, you have to understand a little bit about history. Because there are a whole lot of historical factors that have played a part in our being where we are today, and I think that to even to begin to understand our contemporary issues and contemporary problems, you have to understand a little bit about that history.

Source: Full speech available online at http://snowwowl.com/nativeleaders/wilmaspeech.html.

five-year contract with Harrah's, a national casino-management company, to run their casino, but the tribe continued to operate the tribal bingo hall at another location. The contract awarded Harrah's 27.5 percent of the profit the first year, and this rate declined to 17 percent in the fifth year. Harrah's assumed complete responsibility for the loan required to build the casino, guaranteed the Cherokees $1,000,000 per month profit, promised to donate $400,000 per year for educational programs, agreed to Indian preference in hiring, and established day-care and training programs. So many people packed the casino on opening night that machines ran out of coinage, and managers had to close the doors at midnight. In 2001, the tribe renegotiated its compact with the state to permit an expansion and the next year opened a fifteen-story hotel adjacent to the casino. In November 2003, the Tribal Council approved a new contract with Harrah's that cut the management fee to 8 percent and provided for future reductions that will drop to 5.5 percent of the profit in 2011.

The Eastern Band decided to pay out half of its income from the casino to tribal members. These per-capita payments, as they are called, amounted to about $6,000 per person in 2002. The per-capita payments of children go into trust funds that are available to them at age eighteen if they have graduated from high school; dropouts must wait until they are twenty-one to claim their money. The other half of the income from the casino supports tribal services. Among the many projects funded by gaming money are new sewer and water systems, a fire station, a dialysis facility, and a wellness center. The tribe also has a land-purchase program, and in 2002, it contributed $2.1 million to public service agencies, community groups, and educational institutions.

Gaming has had a major effect on the reservation and the region. By 2002, the casino was a $155-million-a-year business that employed 1,800 people, many of whom were not Cherokees, and paid out more than $48 million in salaries. Local businesses thrived as casino employees bought cars, clothing, and other consumer goods. Tourism, on which the whole region heavily depended, became a year-round enterprise with the casino drawing tourists from across the United States every month of the year. Furthermore, many of the problems that critics had feared before the casino opened did not materialize. Crime even declined because the police department was financially able to add positions and seek better training for its officers. A long-term study of children in western North Carolina revealed that behavioral problems declined markedly after the opening of the casino because their families' improved economic prospects led to less conflict at home and higher self-esteem.

Nevertheless, there are critics of gaming on the reservation and in the surrounding communities. Many people in the region, both Indian and non-Indian, are fundamentalist Christians who oppose gambling on moral grounds. In addition, a number of Cherokee traditionalists have voiced concerns that the enormous influx of non-Indians will result in further loss of cultural values and beliefs. Furthermore, the conviction of two non-Indian operators of the tribal bingo hall on charges of fraud and embezzlement in the mid-1980s made all gaming on the reservation suspect in the view of some.

Gaming also has created political tension. In the early 1990s, the council refused to permit a referendum on gaming, and politicians seemed to be receiving special benefits from a company competing with Harrah's for the casino contract. The voters turned out ten of the twelve council members and elected a new chief, Joyce Dugan, in 1995. Facing impeachment proceedings in the final months of his term, the defeated chief resigned. Since then, the eastern Cherokees have not elected a chief to a second term, an indication of continuing discontent with political leadership on the reservation.

In Oklahoma, the Cherokee Nation has developed gaming enterprises, but they are more modest than those of the Eastern

Band and the effects are less readily apparent. The much larger Cherokee Nation did not have a pre-existing tourist economy, nor does it have a commonly held land base on which most of its members live. At the end of 2003, the Cherokee Nation operated four gaming facilities at Catoosa in the vicinity of Tulsa, Siloam Springs, Roland, and Ft. Gibson. A recent ruling prohibited table games, so these casinos offer only machine games and bingo. The Cherokee Nation does not make per-capita distributions of profits. Instead it uses the income to support education, health care, housing, and community services. In fiscal year 2003, net income from gaming was $38.7 million.

In 2003, the United Keetoowah Band was operating a bingo hall in Tahlequah, Oklahoma, where Cherokee Nation tribal offices are also located, but the future of this facility is in doubt. Oklahoma authorities closed the UKB bingo hall in 2001 because the site was not trust land, that is, the title was not held in trust by the United States. Only trust lands are exempt from state regulatory law and, therefore, legitimate venues for Indian casinos. Members of the United Keetoowah Band and the Cherokee Nation live in the same fourteen counties in northeastern Oklahoma, but the Cherokee Nation has jurisdiction over this territory and must give permission for the UKB to place land in trust. They have declined to do so because they regard such action as an erosion of Cherokee Nation sovereignty. Insisting on their right to operate a gaming facility on property that includes their tribal headquarters, the UKB reopened the bingo hall, and the matter has yet to be resolved legally. This issue is only one of several that has created tension between the two federally recognized Oklahoma Cherokee tribes.

Gaming is not the only economic development project that Cherokees have pursued. In the 1970s, the Cherokee Nation organized Cherokee Nation Industries, which has become a defense contractor that manufactures and distributes components for military hardware ranging from the M-1 Abrams tank to the international space station. Seeking revenue sources in an era of declining federal aid, the Eastern Band purchased a mirror manufacturing firm in 1987, which it sold in 1999. Although mirrors were not made on Qualla Boundary, the profits from the company supported tribal services. Such efforts mean that the tribes are developing diverse economies not solely dependent on gaming.

The tribes have undertaken economic development as an exercise of their sovereignty, that is, the right to govern themselves. The sovereignty of the three Cherokee tribes rests on their formal recognition by the United States government through treaties and legislation. Recognition means that they have a government-to-government relationship with the United States, which has placed the administration of this relationship in the Bureau of Indian Affairs in the Department of the Interior. Although many individuals in the United States claim Cherokee ancestry, they are eligible for the services of the BIA only as enrolled members of the three federally recognized tribes: the Eastern Band of Cherokee Indians, the Cherokee Nation, and the United Keetoowah Band.

In the last two decades of the twentieth century, many groups of people who have Cherokee ancestry have organized as tribes, and some of these groups have received recognition from the states in which they live. The Cherokee Nation and the Eastern Band have opposed the federal recognition of these groups. Federal recognition entails a government-to-government relationship, and these groups do not normally have a history of an organized political or legal existence, that is, a government. Privately, some Cherokees question the Indian ancestry of the members of these groups, which is often (but not always) difficult to document, and their motivation, which frequently seems to stem from some perceived advantage in being Indian.

The United States Supreme Court has upheld the right of Indian tribes to determine their own members, and the basis of citizenship in the three federally recognized tribes is very different. To be a citizen of the Cherokee Nation, a person must descend from someone listed on the Dawes Rolls, which were prepared for allotments and closed in 1906. There is no requirement that a descendant have a particular percentage of Indian ancestry, or "blood quantum." The Eastern Band requires descent from the 1924 Baker Roll and 1/16 blood quantum. The United Keetoowah Band requires descent from their 1950 roll and ¼ blood quantum. Tribal citizenship is a legal definition, therefore, established by each tribe.

A debate over citizenship has emerged within Cherokee tribes. Under the terms of the Reconstruction Treaty of 1866, the former slaves of the Cherokees, or Cherokee freedmen, became citizens of the Cherokee Nation, and in the 1890s, the Dawes Commission drew up a roll of freedmen and issued them allotments. In 1971, Cherokees once again began electing their tribal government, and descendants of freedmen reportedly voted in that election and the subsequent one in 1975. The constitution adopted in 1976, however, limited the franchise to "Cherokees by blood," a provision that precludes descendants of freedmen from voting or holding office. The 2003 constitution did the same. This exclusion of descendants of people whose names appear on the Cherokee freedmen's roll sparked a controversy that is likely to continue for some time.

Unlike the Cherokee Nation whose citizenship stems solely from a historic roll, the Eastern Band of Cherokees has a "blood quantum" requirement as well, and some citizens have questioned the blood quantum of people who appear on their current roll. In 2003, the tribal council considered an audit of the roll to remove individuals who had too much European ancestry, and one council member suggested that all citizens submit to DNA testing, a procedure that medical authorities insist cannot actually reveal race.

Like the members of all communities, Cherokees do not always agree on issues. The most contentious episode in recent Cherokee history took place in Oklahoma in 1997. A justice of the Cherokee Nation Supreme Court issued a warrant for documents in the office of Principal Chief Joe Byrd that the justice believed would reveal the misappropriation of tribal funds. Chief Byrd fired the marshals who seized the documents, and the council impeached the Supreme Court. The court ruled these actions unconstitutional, and so Chief Byrd locked them out of their chambers. Violence erupted in downtown Tahlequah when new marshals appointed by Byrd encountered the marshals recognized by the court, and federal authorities had to restore order. In 1999, the voters spoke by defeating Chief Byrd and electing Chad "Corn Tassel" Smith, a lawyer who had championed the court's position. Smith was reelected in 2003, and a new constitution, which promises to make government more accountable, was also drafted that year.

Even elections, however, have proven problematic at times. One issue that Cherokees debate is absentee ballots. People who may never have lived in North Carolina or Oklahoma but who qualify for citizenship have had voting rights, and their number has grown steadily since the 1950s. Economic and educational opportunities have taken them away, but by voting they continue to play a role in tribal politics, one that some people who reside in tribal communities resent. Many people who vote by absentee ballot, however, actually live within tribal boundaries and simply cannot go to the polls because of age, infirmity, or other obligations. In Oklahoma, some Cherokees vote absentee because they live immediately outside the fourteen county Cherokee Nation—in Ft. Smith, Tulsa, and Fayetteville, for example—but they participate fully in tribal life. Even among Cherokees who live far away, voting tends to be limited to those who keep informed about tribal affairs. Some nonresident Cherokees who have the right to vote

In 2003, Chad "Corn Tassel" Smith was reelected principal chief of the Cherokee Nation. Smith is the great-grandson of Red Bird Smith, a Cherokee patriot who fought against allotment of Cherokee land.

decline to do so because they think it is inappropriate or they do not know enough about the candidates.

In Eastern Band elections in 2003, the absentee vote prompted charges of illegal, unethical, or just unsavory behavior by candidates who tried to appeal to nonresident Cherokees. The incumbent chief, who was one target of these accusations, lost his bid for reelection, and in December 2003, members voted to restrict absentee ballots to those who actually live on the reservation or whose military service or higher education has temporarily taken them away.

The interest that many Cherokees sustain in tribal politics long after they move away from their ancestral communities, however, reflects the deep cultural bond they feel to other Cherokees. Both the Cherokee Nation and the Eastern Band have nurtured that bond in recent years by a renewed emphasis on cultural values. The Cherokee Nation sponsors an adult tribal history course taught in Oklahoma and in Cherokee enclaves from California to Georgia. The tribe also sponsors language courses, and Chief Smith has actively attempted to rekindle gadugi, the spirit of community, which promotes traditional Cherokee culture. The Eastern Band teaches Cherokee history, language, and culture at every grade in its schools. The Eastern Band also used gaming profits to purchase Kituwah, the site of the Cherokees' mother town where they believe they began their existence as a people. Citizens of the Cherokee Nation and the United Keetoowah Band have visited this sacred place, a reminder that although they are distinct tribes today, they share a culture and history.

Friendships and family ties also draw East and West together, and for years Cherokees have traveled hundreds of miles to attend each other's celebrations. In April 1984, a joint council of the Eastern Band of Cherokees and the Cherokee Nation formally assembled at Red Clay, the site where the Cherokees met when Georgia outlawed their government during the removal crisis of the 1830s. In doing so, the tribes reaffirmed the importance of their common heritage. They have held subsequent joint council meetings, and their leaders often appear together at events, including the dedication of a new museum at the Vann house, an early nineteenth-century Cherokee site in North Georgia, and meetings of the Trail of Tears Association, which is dedicated to researching and commemorating removal.

Cherokees, however, are not merely people of the past: They live in the present and they plan for the future. Change and adaptability are a part of their heritage, a persistent theme in their history. When the sons of Kana'ti and Selu could no longer depend on a magical supply of game and vegetables, they learned to hunt and farm. In meeting the challenges of the twenty-first century, modern Cherokees are the true heirs of Kana'ti and Selu. Drawing strength and inspiration from the past, they face the future with confidence. The Cherokees are, after all, the Ani'-Yun'wiya, the principal people.

The Cherokees at a Glance

Tribe Cherokee Nation, Eastern Band of Cherokee Indians, United Keetoowah Band

Culture Area Southeast

Geography Oklahoma, North Carolina

Linguistic Family Iroquoian

Current Population (2000) 220,000 Cherokee Nation of Oklahoma; 12,500 Eastern Band of Cherokee Indians; 10,000 United Keetoowah Band

First European Contact Hernando de Soto, Spanish, 1540

Federal Status Three Federally Recognized Tribes

1540	Europeans first arrive in Cherokee villages, under the command of Hernando de Soto.
1560s	Juan Pardo leads a Spanish expedition to Cherokee territory.
Early eighteenth century	Non-Indian traders begin to build stores in Cherokee territory.
1708	Cherokees sell fifty thousand deerskins to traders.
1735	Because of a sharp rise in demand, Cherokee sales of deerskins to traders increase to one million.
1738	One-third of the Cherokee population dies in a smallpox epidemic.
1754–1763	French and Indian War (called the Seven Years' War in Europe) is fought.
1756	British build Fort Prince George in present-day South Carolina and Fort Loudoun in what is now eastern Tennessee.
1758	Cherokee headmen try to arrange a truce between English settlers and young Cherokee warriors.
1759	Cherokee leaders meet with South Carolina's colonial governor to try to work out a peace agreement to end violence between Europeans and Indians.
1760	Cherokee war chief Oconostota besieges Fort Prince George; in response, British Colonel Archibald Montgomery raids Cherokee territory; the Cherokee force him to retreat; the next summer, British troops raid and destroy Cherokee towns in retaliation.
1770	A treaty takes away Cherokee hunting grounds in Virginia and present-day West Virginia; Sequoyah, the man who developed the Cherokee syllabary, was probably born.
1772	Cherokees give up land east of the Kentucky River.
1775	In a fraudulent transaction, the Cherokees "sell" their land west of the Kentucky River.

1775–1783   American Revolution, in which some Cherokees side with the unsuccessful British, is fought.

1776   Cherokees raid frontiers of Georgia, Virginia, and the Carolinas.

1794   The Chickamaugas (a small band of Cherokees who continued to fight the United States in resistance to forcible relocation) finally decide to seek peace.

1800   Moravians open a mission in Cherokee territory with consent from the tribal council.

1801–1823   U.S. Indian agent Return J. Meigs lives among the Cherokees.

1803   The United States acquires the Louisiana Territory from France.

1808   A council of Cherokee delegates meets and passes a law establishing a police force to protect property; U.S. President Thomas Jefferson tries to convince eastern Indians (including Cherokees) to move west.

1809   Sequoyah begins work on Cherokee syllabary.

1810   U.S. government and Cherokees sign treaty agreeing to a "land exchange."

1817   American Board of Commissioners for Foreign Missions opens a missionary station near present-day Chattanooga, Tennessee; the Cherokees divide their territory into eight electoral districts, each of which sends representatives to the national council.

1817–1819   A number of Cherokees agree to move west in treaty negotiations that promised them compensation from the U.S. government.

1819   Cherokee national council notifies the U.S. government that it will not cede any more land.

1822   The Cherokees establish a supreme court to hear appeals from district courts.

1824   Office of Indian Affairs established.

1827   The Cherokees write a constitution based on that of the United States.

1828–1866   John Ross serves as principal chief of the Cherokees.

1828   The *Cherokee Phoenix* begins publication under editor Elias Boudinot.

1830   Congress passes the Indian Removal Act, allowing the president to negotiate with the Indians for their relocation.

1831   The U.S. Supreme Court rules in *Cherokee Nation* v. *Georgia* that the Cherokee Nation was a domestic dependent nation that had no standing before the Court.

1832   The U.S. Supreme Court rules in *Worcester* v. *Georgia* that the state of Georgia could not impose its laws on the Cherokee Nation.

1835   Treaty of New Echota, providing for the exchange of all Cherokee lands in the Southeast in return for land in northeastern Oklahoma, is negotiated and signed by members of the Treaty Party.

1838–1839   Federal troops round up and force Cherokees to go west over the so-called Trail of Tears from their original homelands to Indian Territory.

1839   Conflict erupts among the different factions of Cherokees in Indian Territory; a majority of the Cherokees unite to write a new constitution, placing the tribe under the leadership of John Ross.

1840s   Cherokees begin to operate a system of public schools.

1844   *Cherokee Advocate* begins publication.

1846   John Ross, Stand Watie, and other Cherokee leaders sign a treaty to end the civil war among factions; the newly unified nation continues to operate under the constitution of 1839.

1851   Two seminaries for Cherokee students open.

1861–1865   American Civil War.

1861   John Ross signs an alliance with the Confederacy.

1862   U.S. forces invade Cherokee territory.

1865   On August 11, the Cherokees sign a treaty granting citizenship to freed slaves, allowing railroads to build on their lands, and making other concessions to the U.S. government.

1868   The Eastern Band of Cherokees write a constitution and elects a chief and council.

1881   Quakers sign a contract with the Eastern Band to set up a school system.

1886   The U.S. Supreme Court rules that the eastern Cherokees had severed their formal ties to the original Cherokee Nation when they refused to move west and therefore had no right to share in the tribe's income.

1887   Congress passes the General Allotment Act (called the Dawes Act), dividing up former tribal lands and parceling them out to individuals in small portions; Cherokees are initially exempted from the act.

1889   The Eastern Band of Cherokees are awarded a corporate charter that will give them some protection under state law.

1890   The federal government closes the so-called Cherokee Strip to white ranchers, cutting off a major source of revenue for the tribe.

1892   The U.S. government takes over the school system set up by the Quakers in Eastern Band Cherokee territory.

1893   Congress directs President Grover Cleveland to have commissioners negotiate for allotment with the Cherokees and other previously exempted peoples; Cherokees are forced to sell the Cherokee Strip to the U.S. government.

1895   A federal court rules that Eastern Band members are not citizens and cannot sell timber on their own land.

1898   Congress passes the Curtis Act, ending Indian land tenure.

1900   The state of North Carolina refuses to allow Cherokees to vote.

1902   With no real option, the Cherokee Nation agrees to allotment.

1905   Cherokees opposed to Oklahoma statehood write a constitution for a proposed state called Sequoyah; Congress rejects the plan and insists that allotment be completed by 1906.

1907   Oklahoma becomes a state.

1914–1918   World War I; the United States joins the war in 1917.

1924   The U.S. government grants citizenship rights to all Native Americans.

1930   Cherokees in North Carolina regain the right to vote.

1934   Great Smoky Mountains National Park opens, making the nearby lands of the Eastern Band a major tourist attraction.

1936   Congress passes the Oklahoma Indian Welfare Act, giving Indians the right to create constitutions and obtain corporate charters.

1939–1945   World War II; the United States enters the war in December 1941 after the Japanese bomb Pearl Harbor.

1946   United Keetoowah Band is federally recognized as a tribe; Cherokee veterans of World War II in North Carolina force county registrars to allow them to vote.

1950   United Keetoowah Band completes its roll of members and constitution and is accepted by the Bureau of Indian Affairs (BIA).

1950s   BIA institutes program encouraging Native Americans to move away from reservations and into urban areas.

1952   The Eastern Band of Cherokees sets up the Cherokee Tribal Community Services program and institutes a sales tax to pay for public services.

1960s   Lyndon Johnson's presidential administration enacts programs called the Great Society aimed at ending poverty in the United States.

1961   The Indian Claims Commission awards the western Cherokee $15 million in recompense for the forced sale of the Cherokee Strip in 1893.

1965–1973   The Five County Northeastern Oklahoma Cherokee Organization calls attention to the difficult lives of traditional Cherokees and demands that Cherokee leaders include them in development plans.

1971   Citizens of the Cherokee Nation vote for principal chief for the first time since Oklahoma became a state in 1907.

1976   The Cherokee Nation writes a new constitution providing for the election of tribal officials.

1982   Eastern Cherokees open a lucrative bingo parlor.

1984   A joint council of the Eastern Band and Cherokee Nation holds a meeting to reaffirm the importance of their common cultural heritage.

1985   Wilma Mankiller is elected the first female principal chief of the Cherokee Nation.

1987   U.S. Supreme Court rules that if a state permits any type of gambling, then Indian casinos there are legal; The following year, Congress passes the Indian Gaming Regulatory Act, requiring reservations to negotiate with states in order to have certain types of casino operations.

1990   The United Keetoowah Band prohibits dual tribal membership for all newly enrolled members.

1997   A justice of the Cherokee Nation Supreme Court has Chief Joe Byrd arrested on charges of misappropriating tribal funds.

1999   Voters respond to the case against Byrd by electing Chad "Corn Tassel" Smith to replace him as principal chief.

2001   Eastern Band of Cherokees renegotiate their contract with North Carolina to expand their casino operation.

2002   Eastern Band opens a new hotel next to its casino; the tribe begins per-capita payments to tribal members.

2003   The Eastern Band Tribal Council negotiates with Harrah's casinos for a deal that will reduce Harrah's share of profits; Chad Smith reelected principal chief of Cherokee Nation.

acculturation—The process by which cultures change when they come in contact with one another.

allotment—U.S. policy adopted in the General Allotment Act of 1887, intended to assimilate Indians by breaking up tribally owned reservations and assigning small tracts to individual Indians.

asi—Cherokee winter houses of wattle and daub construction with a hearth in the center of the room.

black drink—An herbal beverage used by tribes throughout the Southeast as part of a purification ritual.

Booger Dance—A dance performed by the Cherokees in which they expressed their views on the essential natures of other peoples.

Bureau of Indian Affairs (BIA)—A U.S. government agency assigned to the Department of the Interior in 1849. It replaced an office in the War Department that had managed trade and other relations with Indians. The BIA provides services, such as education and health care, to federally recognized tribes, not to individuals. In the twenty-first century, the BIA increasingly provides funds to tribes that then contract for these services.

clan—A multigenerational group that descends from a common, often mythical, ancestor. Because clan members consider themselves closely related, they strictly prohibit marriage within the clan. Cherokees determine clan membership by matrilineal descent.

General Allotment or Dawes Act—An 1887 federal law that divided reservation land into 160-acre farms and assigned them to individual Indians, who were then required to give up tribal practices and become American citizens.

Green Corn Ceremony—An annual celebration of purification, forgiveness, and thanksgiving held when the new crop of corn became edible.

Homestead Act—An 1862 federal law that granted 160 acres of land to any head of a family who agreed to cultivate the land for five years.

Indian Gaming Regulatory Act—A law passed in 1988 that gives the federal government oversight of Indian gaming operations.

Indian Removal Act—An 1830 federal law that authorized the president of the United States to negotiate the removal of eastern Indian tribes to new lands west of the Mississippi River.

GLOSSARY

Indian Reorganization Act— A 1934 federal law that ended the policy of allotment and provided for political and economic development of reservation communities.

matrilineal; matrilineality— A principle of descent by which kinship is traced through female ancestors; the basis for Cherokee clan membership.

matrilocal residence— A tradition in which a married couple lives with or near the wife's mother's family.

Proclamation of 1763— A royal decree of Britain's King George III prohibiting colonists from settling west of the Appalachian Mountains and reserving this area for Indians.

removal policy— A federal policy formulated in 1830 that called for the resettlement of Indians from eastern and southern states west of the Mississippi River.

reservation— A tract of land set aside by treaty for the occupation and use by Indians; also called a reserve. Some reservations were for an entire tribe; others were for individual Indians.

Trail of Tears— The harsh journey of Cherokees forced out of their homeland in the Southeast by the federal government to their relocation site in what is now Oklahoma.

treaty— A legal agreement negotiated between representatives of sovereign governments. Until 1871, when Congress brought the practice to a halt, the United States and Indian nations conducted their relationship through treaties.

trust land— Land whose title is held by the U.S. government for use by Indians and over which the United States, rather than the states, has jurisdiction.

Books

Anderson, William L. *Cherokee Removal: Before and After*. Athens, Ga.: University of Georgia Press, 1991.

Duncan, Barbara R., and Brett H. Riggs. *Cherokee Heritage Trails Guidebook*. Chapel Hill, N.C.: University of North Carolina Press, 2003.

Finger, John R. *Cherokee Americans: The Eastern Band of Cherokees in the Twentieth Century*. Lincoln, Nebr.: University of Nebraska Press, 1991.

————. *The Eastern Band of Cherokees, 1819–1900*. Knoxville, Tenn.: University of Tennessee Press, 1984.

Hatley, M. Thomas. *The Dividing Paths: Cherokees and South Carolinians through the Era of Revolution*. New York: Oxford University Press, 1993.

Hicks, Hannah. "The Diary of Hannah Hicks." *American Scene* 13 (1972).

Malone, Henry Thompson. *Cherokees of the Old South: A People in Transition*. Athens, Ga.: University of Georgia Press, 1956.

Mankiller, Wilma Pearl, and Michael Wallis. *Mankiller: A Chief and Her People*. New York: St. Martin's Press, 1994.

McLoughlin, William G. *After the Trail of Tears: The Cherokees' Struggle for Sovereignty, 1839–1880*. Chapel Hill, N.C.: University of North Carolina Press, 1993.

————. *Cherokee Renascence in the New Republic*. Princeton, N.J.: Princeton University Press, 1986.

Moutlon, Gary E. *John Ross, Cherokee Chief*. Athens, Ga.: University of Georgia Press, 1985.

Oakley, Christopher Arris. "Indian Gaming and the Eastern Band of Cherokee Indians," *North Carolina Historical Review* 78 (2001): 133–55.

Perdue, Theda. *Cherokee Women: Gender and Culture Change, 1700–1835*. Lincoln, Nebr.: University of Nebraska Press, 1998.

————. "Letters from Brainerd," *Journal of Cherokee Studies* 4 (1979): 4–9.

————. *Nations Remembered: An Oral History of the Five Civilized Tribes, 1865–1907*. Westport, Conn.: Greenwood, 1980.

———. *Slavery and the Evolution of Cherokee Society, 1540–1866.* Knoxville, Tenn.: University of Tennessee Press, 1979.

———, and Michael D. Green. *The Cherokee Removal.* New York: Bedford Books, 1995.

Satz, Ronald N. *American Indian Policy in the Jacksonian Era.* Lincoln, Nebr.: University of Nebraska Press, 1976.

Strickland, Rennard. *Fire and the Spirits: Cherokee Law from Clan to Court.* Norman, Okla.: University of Oklahoma Press, 1982.

Sturm, Circe. *Blood Politics: Race, Culture, and Identity in the Cherokee Nation of Oklahoma.* Berkeley, Calif.: University of California Press, 2002.

Websites

All Things Cherokee
http://www.allthingscherokee.com/

The Cherokee Cultural Society of Houston
http://www.powersource.com/cherokee/

Cherokee Heritage Center
http://www.cherokeeheritage.org/

Cherokee Tribal Archives Project
http://www.rootsweb.com/~cherokee/

Chronicles of Oklahoma, A History of the Cherokee Indians
http://www.digital.library.okstate.edu/chronicles/v008/v008p407.html

The Official Home Page of the Eastern Band of Cherokee Indians
http://www.cherokee-nc.com/

Official Site of the Cherokee Nation
http://www.cherokee.org/

page:

2:	Library of Congress Map Division	85:	© Annie Griffiths Belt/CORBIS
24:	© Smithsonian Institution National Anthropological Archives	95:	Associated Press, AP
37:	Library of Congress, LC-USZC4-2566	103:	Courtesy of Principal Chief Chad Smith
47:	Library of Congress, LC-USZC4-3156	A:	© Smithsonian Institution
53:	Library of Congress	B:	© Richard A. Cooke/CORBIS
55:	Library of Congress, LC-USZC4-3157	C:	© Smithsonian Institution
61:	© Medford Historical Society/CORBIS	D:	© Bettmann/CORBIS
64:	Library of Congress Map Division	E:	© Richard A. Cooke/CORBIS
80:	© Smithsonian Institution	F:	© Raymond Gehman/COBIS
		G:	© Art Resource, NY
		H:	© Richard A. Cooke/CORBIS

Cover: © Richard A. Cooke/CORBIS

Theda Perdue is Professor of History and American Studies at the University of North Carolina. In addition to *The Cherokees*, her published work includes *Slavery and the Evolution of Cherokee Society, 1540–1865* (1979), *Nations Remembered: An Oral History of the Five Civilized Tribes* (1980), *Cherokee Editor* (1983), *Native Carolinians* (1985), *Cherokee Women: Gender and Culture Change, 1700–1835* (1998), *Sifters: Native American Women's Lives* (2001), *The Columbia Guide to American Indians of the Southeast* (2001), and *"Mixed Blood" Indians: Racial Construction in the Early South* (2003).

Ada E. Deer is the director of the American Indian Studies program at the University of Wisconsin-Madison. She was the first woman to serve as chair of her tribe, the Menominee Nation, the first woman to head the Bureau of Indian Affairs in the U.S. Department of the Interior, and the first American Indian woman to run for Congress and secretary of state of Wisconsin. Deer has also chaired the Native American Rights Fund, coordinated workshops to train American Indian women as leaders, and championed Indian participation in the Peace Corps. She holds degrees in social work from Wisconsin and Columbia.